Death Fucking Sucks

Dan Borchers

Published by Kingborch Ink
ISBN: 979-8-9991352-0-9 (Paperback)
Cover design by Dan Borchers
Interior formatting by the author with assistance from editorial AI technology in an editorial support capacity only.

Printed in the United States of America
First Edition: 2025

For rights inquiries, media requests, or speaking engagements, contact:
info@kingborchink.com

"There's no book for this sort of thing…"
                              -Travis Lee Gutierrez

Challenge accepted Trav.

This book is dedicated to any and every person in the ocean of grief. I see you.

Acknowledgements

To everyone who's ever stood at a gravesite, stared at the ceiling at 3:30 a.m., or screamed into a steering wheel—you're the reason this book exists.

This isn't the kind of book you write alone. It's the result of a lifetime of loss, love, loyalty, and all the brutal shit in between.

To my family—those still here, and those who left too soon—thank you for shaping me, breaking me, and teaching me that grief isn't weakness. It's proof we loved hard.

To Travis—my brother in every way that mattered. Your story runs through every page of this. You showed me what friendship looks like when it's real, and what absence feels like when it's permanent. This book carries your name, even if it doesn't spell it out.

To Melissa—you walked beside me through the deepest shadows and still saw light in me. Thank you for reminding me I'm more than my pain, and for pushing me to reclaim the parts of myself I thought were lost—my voice, my art, my words. You didn't just love who I was… you believed in who I could still become.

To my kids—you are why I keep going. I hope one day you read this and understand that healing isn't about pretending to be okay. It's about choosing to keep living even when the world goes quiet.

To Chidley and my best friends who answered late-night texts, showed up without needing a reason, or simply sat with me in the silence—you helped carry this weight.

And to grief itself—fuck you but thank you. You hollowed me out, but you also made room for something new.

Finally, to anyone holding broken pieces of themselves: I hope these pages help you realize you're not alone. That your pain is valid. That survival isn't soft. And that even when death fucking sucks—life, somehow, still finds a way forward.

This book is for you.

—Dan Borchers

Prologue

Death fucking sucks. Let's start there.

I remember the first time I looked grief in the eye - the following hush of the funeral home, the stale coffee nobody wanted, the way my heartbeat thundered in my ears even though the entire room seemed stuck on mute. And that's the thing about grief: there's no neat trick, no magic formula to flip the switch and make it go away. So if you picked up this book hoping for a gentle self-help guide, you might want to set it down now.

Because this isn't a self-help book. It's not a 10-step manual on how to "get over" grief. It's not soft, it's not cute, and it sure as hell isn't clean. This is a book about grief in all its messy, ugly, raw, and sometimes darkly funny forms. I'm talking about the kind of grief that punches you in the gut when you think you're finally okay, the kind that invades your dreams and leaves you gasping for air in the middle of the night.

It's about the grief from death.
Losing people while they're still alive.
Burying dreams, you swore would last forever.
Watching marriages dissolve right before your eyes.
Mourning your old self as you become someone new.

I'm no psychologist. I don't have a PhD, and I damn sure don't have a grief counseling certificate. Hell, I barely scraped together enough college credits to call it an associate's degree. But what I do have is a long-ass list of funerals, heartbreaks, breakdowns, and the kind of losses that don't come with a user manual. I know what it's like to sit in a parked car, tears flooding your vision while the engine's still running, wondering if you'll ever catch your breath again.

Yet somehow, in the aftermath of all that shit, I built a life. I'm a multi-unit leader in a Fortune Top 50 company, which is a fancy way of saying I've had to keep my head on straight while leading up to a hundred employees at any given time. That means I've had to guide others through their own storms while my own personal waves kept crashing over me. I learned pretty quickly that pretending to be okay isn't the same as being okay. And I found out that vulnerability—raw, unfiltered vulnerability—isn't a weakness. It's the only damn bridge to connection and purpose when everything else feels like it's falling apart.

This book is my truth.
My observations.
My scars, my sarcasm, my soul.

There will be dark humor—because sometimes laughter is the only rope you can cling to before the floodwaters drag you under. There will be physics references and comic book analogies— because, trust me, even Spandex-wearing heroes know a thing or two about grief. Some stories might rip your chest open; others might glide over you without leaving a mark.

And that's okay, because this isn't a measuring contest of who's hurting the most. None of us are special in that regard. Pain is pain. Loss is loss.

Our stories are all unique, and that's what makes us not special. Grief binds us, even if our losses look different. If sharing my journey helps you feel a little less alone in yours, then every dark night I've endured matters in a whole new way.

Grief is like the ocean: it never fully goes away. You're forced to learn how to sail, to read the tide, to brace yourself when the undertow grabs at your ankles. Over time, you figure out how to stay afloat—even when the storm hits. Sometimes, if you're lucky, you'll learn how to glide across those swells with a fleeting sense of peace.

And I hope this book becomes the wind in your sails. A steady push of perspective and presence when you feel lost on those endless waters. Because I've been there—adrift, terrified, clinging to a busted piece of driftwood that I prayed would keep me breathing until morning.

During one of the deaths you'll read about, my brother told me something that stuck: "Maybe you had to go through this so you could guide the rest of us when it's our turn." At first, it felt like a cruel trade—pain for purpose. I hated the idea that my heartbreak might serve as someone else's lesson plan.

But in time, I realized he might be right. Because I've navigated these waters enough to spot the rip currents hidden dangers just under the water surface you never see coming. And if I can be your guide and shine a little light on those treacherous spots, if I can say, "You're going to hate this stretch, but you'll survive it," then maybe it's worth it.

Most of my life, I didn't feel like I had sails. No map, no compass, no wind—just me, alone in a leaky boat, rowing like hell through waters I couldn't understand. If you know that feeling—if your arms are tired and your heart's even more exhausted—this book is for you because you're not alone anymore. We're sailing together

1
The Marine

"The more precisely the position is determined, the less precisely the momentum is known." — Werner Heisenberg

Jeffery Allen Borchers was my uncle. A Lance Corporal in the United States Marines. The second oldest of my grandparents' five children. My mom was the oldest. I was just two years old when he died—too young to remember him, but not too young to inherit the shadow his death cast over the rest of us.

Grief became our only family heirloom. Like a shitty version of Thor's hammer heavy as hell, impossible to lift unless you were worthy. Only our worthiness wasn't measured by nobility or courage, but by how many funerals we could stomach without falling apart.

That Heisenberg quote above? It's not just physics. It's prophecy. It explains what Jeff's death did to our family. Random. Unforeseen. Violent. Like a perfect storm colliding with fragile coordinates. One second you think you're grounded, and the next, you're free-falling through a reality you didn't choose. That's the thing about grief—it turns time and space inside out. You lose track of direction, of meaning. One moment, everything is steady. The next, the bottom falls out, and you're left in a story with no clear beginning or end.

My grandpa—our patriarch—was no stranger to that kind of story. He knew trauma before he had the language for it. When he was just four or five, he watched his own father die in a farming accident in Iowa. A tractor. Steel and engine versus flesh and blood. That kind of image brands itself into a boy's bones. His mother eventually remarried, brought a stepfather into the picture, and life marched on. But grief had already planted itself in him, coiling deep in his chest. And like so many men of his era, he never spoke about it.

Instead, he enlisted. Navy. Vietnam. His mother made his brothers enlist, too.
"If he's going to war," she said, "you're going with him. You're going to protect each other."

Even as a kid, hearing that struck something primal in me. It embedded the idea of brotherhood, of unity, into my DNA. That if one of us goes to war, we all go. That loyalty doesn't wait for convenience. It just shows up.

After the war, my grandpa came home. Met Janice—who went by Jan, my grandmother—and started a family. My mom came first, then Uncle Jeff, followed by Aunt Kim, Uncle B.J, and Uncle Chad. They carved out a life together. Grandpa built a drywall business from the ground up—hands that once held rifles now shaping homes. His skill was legend. Art pulled from mud and plaster. People came from across the country to learn from him. He was even invited to teach at a college overseas in Germany because he was a man who could shape a wall into perfection with just a trowel and a little patience.

When I was little, I saw the results: the big house, the nice vehicles, the garage full of power and pride. This was a man who had made something from nothing. A man who didn't flinch at hard things—because he had already survived the hardest.

But trauma never really leaves. It just buries itself beneath fresh coats of paint.

In the 1970s, their four-year-old son, Chad, was diagnosed with leukemia. War didn't end when my grandpa came home; it just changed shape. The enemy became cancer. Grief became the new battleground. Survival meant something completely different.

There was no pause button. No grace period. My grandpa had to keep the business running, keep food on the table for five kids. While his son was dying, he was up at dawn, grinding on job sites, trying to be both father and provider—heartbreak and hammer swinging in rhythm.

He went to the hospital when he could, but most of the care fell on my grandma. And she didn't just step up—she went to war for her son. She scoured for hope anywhere it could be found. She once told me how she tried to take Chad to either Colorado or Louisiana—I can't remember which—where some experimental treatment was being done. It was so new, so risky, it wasn't even technically legal. She risked arrest for a shot at saving him. She didn't blink.

And in the final moments of his life—when most four-year-olds are thinking about cartoons or candy—Chad looked up at her with eyes too wise for his age and whispered:

"It's okay. I'm ready to see Jesus now."

That sentence cracked her open and anchored her all at once. It broke something in her—but it also planted something. A seed of faith that would bloom in the dark.

She clung to her evangelical Christianity after that.

My grandpa? He clung to work. Duty. Stoicism. A God-and-country man through and through. Not loud about his pain, but always the first in and the last out. He taught us to show up. To grind. To endure. That kind of resilience becomes generational.

Jeff soaked it all in, being the golden son.

The baseball star, just like his dad. My grandpa had the high school record for the most home runs in a season. His name was still on the wall when I visited the school in 2002. A sport that only brought them closer together.

Jeff was charismatic, magnetic, and all-around athletic. Charming as hell. Movie-star handsome. The kind of guy you wanted on your team and by your side. His dream? The Secret Service—he wanted to protect the President. Maybe it was something in the bloodline, that immigrant fire still pulsing through us from our Swedish great-grandfather, the first born on American soil. Or maybe it was just Jeff being Jeff.

So, he joined the Marines.

Boot camp. Graduation. He made it. And then, like a cosmic joke, the universe handed him paradise: Hawaii. That lucky son of a bitch. The kind of assignment you almost don't believe until your boots hit the tarmac.

I picture him stepping off the plane. Pacific air thick and warm, wrapping around him like a blanket woven in salt and sunshine. The scent of coconuts drifting on the breeze. Skin kissed gold by the sun. The sound of waves crashing not far from the base. Nights filled with two giant, beautiful moons—one suspended in the velvet Hawaiian sky, the other shimmering softly across the ocean's surface, reflecting dreams and possibilities Jeff had only just begun to touch.

And for the first time, maybe ever, he could breathe.

He had made it out.

Out of the grief. Out of the weight of a family trying to hold itself together.

He was building something new. Something hopeful. And when someone in the family finds that kind of freedom, even just a taste, it makes the rest of us believe—maybe we can make it, too.

My mom once told me about the first thing Jeff said to her after my brother Bobby was born. He shook his head, laughing, and teased, "Keep having kids at this rate and you'll end up an old lady living in a shoe!" He didn't know Josh and Megan would arrive in the mid-90s. He definitely didn't know AOL was coming or that my mom would choose *"oldladyinashoe"* as her AOL screen name. He just laughed—eyes bright with mischief, teasing his big sister while breathing air tinged with salt, half a world away in paradise.

Back home in Iowa, in a city surrounded by fields of corn, things were… functioning.

Grandpa's business was booming. There were grandkids now— me, my brother, cousin Emily. The family tree had new branches. But underneath it all, the roots were still cracked.

My grandpa never dealt with Chad's death. He buried it in joint compound and job estimates. And the thing about burying grief is, once you start, you don't stop. You bury one heartbreak, and the rest follow. He missed signs. My mom and her siblings didn't finish high school. My mom had me at twenty. My aunt had her first child at sixteen. No one had a map. No one was steering the ship.

Grandpa just kept working. Distracted by grief. By drugs. By gambling. By anything that kept his hands full and his heart numb.

He was building a legacy—but the foundation was cracked.

Still, Jeff seemed to rise above it. He was the one. The one who made it out clean.

The Marine.
The protector.
The future.

And then one ordinary day in March, a car turned down the long gravel road toward the house on Talbot Road.

My grandpa heard it before he saw it.
Tires crunching stone. A sound that shouldn't have meant anything—until it did.

Two Marines sat quietly in the car, dressed in their Service A uniforms—green coats pressed sharp, khaki shirts buttoned tight, covers resting in their laps. There was a stillness to them, a discipline carved into every line of their posture. No words. No glances. Just the steady presence of men carrying out a sacred, gut-wrenching duty. When they finally parked and stepped out, they moved with intention. Jackets adjusted. Covers placed.

Faces unreadable. Then, without hesitation, they walked toward the door.

And delivered the kind of news that guts a family from the inside out. News no one prepares for. No one survives without changing.

Jeff wasn't just dead.

He had been murdered.

2

3:30 AM

In a lot of spiritual traditions, 3:30 AM carries weight. Some say it's when the veil between this world and the next thins out—when spirits whisper, when truth slips through the cracks in silence. In Vedic philosophy, it's called Brahma Muhurta, the Divine Hour—a time for clarity, meditation, presence. And maybe that's all bullshit. Or maybe it's not. But some believe if you wake up around that time, it's not coincidence. It's because something—or someone—is trying to reach you.

For my family, 3:30 AM wasn't mystical. It was the moment everything fucking shattered.

That was the exact time we lost Jeff.

He was supposed to be off duty that night. He had leave coming up and planned to visit us—me, my grandpa, my grandma. I was two. That trip would've been the first time I truly met him, the first real memory I could've carried of the man who represented hope in a legacy cracking under the weight of its own grief.

But hope and timing don't always shake hands. Whether it was fate, bad luck, or some goddamn cosmic glitch—it doesn't matter. What matters is that night, everything changed.

One of the other sentries had called in sick. And in true Borchers fashion, when someone needed help, Jeff stepped up. He raised his hand. Volunteered to take the shift.

Back then, guard duty wasn't a chair behind bulletproof glass. It wasn't air conditioning and coffee. It was a post. A gun. A path. You walked—back and forth—all night. Alone. Eyes up. Watching IDs. Watching shadows.

Gate Post 19—now renamed Borchers Gate—sat just outside the Pacific Fleet headquarters at Pearl Harbor. It should've been uneventful. Just another quiet watch under the stars.

But at 3:30 in the fucking morning, two civilians approached. Wendell Pichay distracted him while Herman Kua II circled behind. Their motive? Stupidity and ego. They wanted to brag that they'd taken a Marine's sidearm. That's what my grandma always told me—they wanted the gun. The uniform. The power.

Jeff probably saw them coming—two dark silhouettes emerging from shadows under the harsh glare of floodlights. He likely tensed, fingers tightening around his weapon, heart pounding as adrenaline surged. His breath caught in his chest. He didn't know them, didn't know their story. Just two strangers stepping out of the dark. And before instinct could take over, before training could kick in, the night exploded into fire and sound. Six shots. Six jolts. Then silence.

In those ten seconds, they took his life, stole their trophy, upended a family—and ran.

The FBI and Naval Investigative Service launched a full-blown investigation. At first, they assumed it was internal—a fight or dispute that had turned Marine against Marine. They questioned his unit, his roommates, his friends. But slowly, the pieces aligned. The truth came into focus.

On May 25, 1990, after a six-hour standoff, Pichay was arrested. He was later convicted and sentenced to life in prison without the possibility of parole. Kua, who testified against him, got seventeen years.

The story was big enough that the History Channel aired a full hour-long episode of The Real NCIS about it years later.

But that's all the world ever saw—the headline, the episode, the true crime story.

What we lived was the fallout.

After Jeff died, our family table got quieter, emptier. Thanksgivings, once overflowing with laughter, teasing, the clink of glasses and the smack of plates, became hushed, strained. Every missing voice became a silent scream. Christmas mornings grew hollow—stockings untouched, tree lights dimmer. Jeff's absence didn't just linger. It echoed.

And grief didn't just sit on my grandpa's shoulders. It devoured him from the inside out.

At first, he did what he always did—buried it. Tried to be strong. Pretended. Powered through. But that kind of pain? You can't outwork it forever. Not when your boy's blood stains paradise.

So he drank.
He gambled.
He numbed.

And slowly, he lost everything.

The business. Gone.

The marriage. Gone.
He was arrested. Then again. And again.

Every time it looked like he might claw his way back, life—or pain—kicked him back down. The man who once had a garage full of tools and the newest Chevy or Ford in the driveway was now patching together clunkers with duct tape—if he had a car at all.

But with me? He smiled.

He was still funny as hell. The life of the party when he let himself be. He taught me how to carry myself, how to laugh through struggle, how to be a man even when the world was falling apart. He tried. He really did. But sometimes… that light in him dimmed. And when it did, the grief lashed out.

Not usually at us grandkids—but at his own kids. The silence could scream. The words could cut. He didn't know how to process it. No one had ever taught him how to feel. So he just… hurt. And in hurting, he hurt others.

He read his Bible. Sat in church pews. Searched for meaning in hymns, worship, and scripture. But no verse, no song, no sermon brought Chad or Jeff back. Nothing made the pain logical. Nothing made it stop.

He had survived so much already—war, loss, heartbreak—but the murder of his son was different. That single act didn't just crack him. It split everything wide open. It was the action that set off a goddamn tidal wave. And the reaction was brutal—a family bursting apart, crashing into the cliffside, fractured at the core.

The big Thanksgivings ended. The noisy Christmases faded. The chaos of a packed house full of warmth and clamor gave way to cold silence.

WIC checks. Food stamps. Stretching dollars, praying to make it another week. Watching a man who once stood ten feet tall struggle to stand at all. And we all saw it. We watched him slip further under. Quietly. Painfully. Drowning in memory, in regret, in silence.

And the worst part?

The current started pulling us down with him.

Thankfully, I had a few anchors that held. One in particular—my great-grandpa—still showed up as a male role model strong enough to keep me from being completely dragged under.

Fred Carlson.

My great-grandfather. My grandmother's dad. A quiet giant with hands like oak and a soul carved from the immigrant grit of his Swedish parents. He was the first in our family born on American soil. Hardship in his bones. Pride in his heart.

Fred didn't say much. He didn't have to. When he sat beside you, you felt steadied. When he looked at you, you felt seen. He was presence. He was peace. He was gravity when everything else was floating away.

He showed me what resilience could look like when it didn't roar—but stood its ground. And that mattered. Because grief? Grief is relentless. It snaps chains. It wears down anchors. It hollows out even the strongest.

Because when death rolls in uninvited, violent, and chaotic, it doesn't just claim a single life. It steals breath from a bloodline, drowns generations, and leaves survivors gasping for air—clinging desperately to whatever anchors remain.

3

The Women Who Raised Me

Before the world pulled me under—before silence moved in and never fully left—there were women who helped me stand. I didn't know it then, but they were planting things inside me. Resilience. My voice. Fire. The kind of tools you don't even realize you're holding until the world falls apart and you're still standing.

In the '90s, while other kids had the classic "mom and dad" setup—or maybe bounced between split homes—I was being raised by a small, mighty army of women. Strong, soulful, steel spined women who knew how to survive, build, and love through the grind. I didn't just have a mom. I also had a grandma and a stepmom who never once felt like a step anything. Brick by brick, these three women laid the foundation I stand on. They shaped the way I move through this world, especially when it tries to break me.

My mom had me young. She was twenty years old, waiting tables while pregnant. That blows my fucking mind to this day. I know twenty-year-olds who can't even decide what shoes to wear.
There she was, carrying plates and life, all while holding onto dreams she couldn't fully chase. She had no safety net. No savior. Just her grit, her God, and her grind.

Growing up, most days were held together by duct tape and prayer. Through the screams of babies and toddlers, messes, piles of laundry, and dirt as a yard it was still home.

There was order. Discipline. Heat in the furnace and heat in the love. She didn't play. She leaned into the church, into community, into structure. Because when the world feels like chaos, sometimes rules are the only support beams keeping the roof from caving in.

Our house wasn't cold. It was firm but never void of warmth.
She hugged with intention. Prayed with fire.
And she made room for all of us—three boys and a girl—without flinching.
Most of the dads were either gone or lost in their own bullshit.
So she stepped in. She didn't just fill the gaps—she became the entire bridge.

No matter how tight money was—and trust me, it was tight—she somehow made Christmas feel huge. We didn't have much, but every Christmas morning felt like magic. Whether it was a Super Nintendo, an Xbox, or something equally mind-blowing, she always pulled it off. We never knew how—at least not until years later, when we discovered the secret magic was called layaway at Kmart. She made us believe in miracles, even if they were the kind you paid off five bucks at a time.

And I'll say it loud: I owe my work ethic to her.

Watching her show up, day after day, holding it all together when everything around her was falling apart… it carved that ethic into my bones. Even now, when I hit a wall, I can hear her in my head: "You keep going."

She taught me the cost of survival. She taught me that showing up isn't just something you do when you feel like it—it's something you do because people are counting on you.

But she wasn't the only one who raised me.

There was my grandma—my mom's mom. Some of my earliest memories have her in them. Long drives. Fishing trips. Her laughter floating through the car windows like music.

She loved cooking and baking—it was her way of bringing us together, no matter how broken or scattered we were. Maybe that's why years later I found myself drawn to baking too, kneading dough or mixing batter just to feel close to her again.

I was five years old when Grandma first gave me a cup of black coffee—bitter, strong, and about as subtle as a slap to the face. And while today I still enjoy my basic-bitch caramel macchiato from Starbucks, there's something grounding in the simplicity of plain black coffee. It reminds me of her quiet pride, of mornings spent at her kitchen table, learning resilience one careful sip at a time.

She carried her faith like a lantern. But she also knew how to find the humor in life. She knew that holiness could be found in belly laughs and dirty hands. She didn't just survive grief—she walked with it, head high, back straight.

After losing not one but two sons, she still showed up. Still hosted holidays. Still made room at the table for people shunned by society but had no business being left out.

She showed me how to carry pain without weaponizing it. How to lead by love. That being the oldest wasn't about power—it was about responsibility.

Her strength didn't scream. It didn't need to.
It lived in her presence.

She taught me that showing up for others, even when you're wounded, is holy work.

And then there was Diane.

If my mom was the anchor and my grandma was the tide that kept me steady, Diane was the spark on the horizon—the glint of sunlight dancing on the waves, reminding me there was still something beautiful ahead.

Even beyond being an incredible mother figure, she was the bridge to my dad's side of the family. She didn't have to be. But she chose to be.

She kept me close to my other grandmother. My aunts. My cousins. She made sure that connection—the one that could've easily snapped—stayed alive.

Sometimes she'd bring over my cousin Anthony—Ant—or his sister Jennifer just so we could hang out. Other times, she'd send me to their place, keeping the thread of family stitched together even when everything else felt like it was coming undone.

Ant and I were close. But we were young adolescent boys who had our own chip on our shoulders, so yeah—we fought.
Big. Loud. Stupid fights.
But Diane didn't let us just slam doors and stew in silence. She made us sit in it. Made us talk it out. Not with yelling—but with presence. With truth.

And when Diane said she was disappointed?
That shit hit harder than any punishment ever could.

Because she believed in you.

She saw the best in you, and when you fell short of that, it felt like you'd let something sacred down.

She didn't just keep us connected—she kept us accountable.

After she married my dad, most people would call her my stepmom.
But to me? She was just another mom.
Another lighthouse in the fog.

Diane had a way of seeing what others overlooked. One summer, when I was seven, I'd been limping for days. I tried hiding it because that's what boys did—grit their teeth and kept going. But Diane noticed.

"Danny, come here. What's wrong with your foot?" Her voice was gentle but firm, eyes concerned and searching. I told her something was hurting my toe. She sat me down, took a careful look, and sighed deeply. It was badly infected—a large cyst had formed around a sliver I hadn't even known was there.

She handed me something soft to squeeze, knelt in front of me, and looked me straight in the eyes. "Danny, this is really going to hurt, bud. I'm not trying to hurt you, but if we don't take care of this now, it'll get worse. Do you understand?"

I nodded nervously, and she squeezed. Pain shot through me, sharp and sudden, tears burning down my face. But she didn't let go until it was done. Of all the adults around me, she was the only one who saw the wound—both the one on my foot and the one hidden deeper—and gently, bravely helped me heal it. Diane didn't just tell me pain was part of life; she showed me how to face it with grace.

She saw me—really saw me—during a time when I was lost in my own skin.
She leaned in when I got quiet. She
asked the hard questions. She listened
with her whole heart.

She made it okay to feel things.
She made it okay to ask questions.
She taught me that curiosity isn't a weakness—it's a tool for loving people better.

She believed in voice. And when I was quiet, she didn't ignore it—she pulled me closer.

Her love wasn't loud, but it was powerful. She was proof that you don't have to give birth to someone to mother them.

These three women—my mom, my grandma, Diane—they were my Avengers. My real-life Marvel™ lineup.
Each with their own origin story. Each with powers that kept me alive.

My mom?
She was more like Jessica Jones—tough as hell, no time for bullshit, and powered by something deeper than just strength. She didn't wear a cape or ask for credit. She carried the weight of the world in silence, fought battles no one saw, and still managed to show up to every school event like it was sacred.

My grandma?
Professor X. Quiet wisdom. Spiritual strength.
She led from the back of the room, lifting others with grace and calm. Her presence made you feel like you mattered. Because to her—you did.

And Diane?

Storm. Voice like thunder. Spirit like lightning.

She moved with grace but never dulled her strength. She didn't just walk into rooms—she changed their temperature. She taught me that softness and power can exist in the same breath.

They weren't perfect. They didn't have capes or theme songs.

But they were my heroes.

Maybe that's why I still work a little harder every time I have a woman as a leader.

Not out of guilt. Out of instinct. Out of respect.

It's not conscious—it's ancestral. It's in my muscle memory.

It's in the rhythm of my survival.

And it wasn't just them. There were others.

Aunt Kim, who would let me move in later when the world got heavy.

Ginnie, who lit a fire for art and imagination.

Shirley, the neighbor who tried to teach me piano before life hit fast-forward.

Clara, who was my babysitter and taught me to look at someone from inside and that skin color has nothing to do with someone's character. That food brings people together and that it should be full of flavor.

They weren't replacements; they were reinforcements—
extensions of the foundation laid by my mom, my grandma, and
Diane, each adding layers of strength, warmth, and courage.
Each one left fingerprints on my soul.

If my mom taught me that faith gets you through the dark,
My grandma taught me that connection carries you across it,
And Diane taught me that your voice might just save you.

None of them were saints. But they are my superheroes. And I
carry them with me. Every day. In the way I lead. In the way I
speak. In the way I survive.

People ask me all the time: How have you kept going? How do
you keep showing up?

This is how.

Because they taught me.

To stand.
To speak.
To love—even when it hurts.

To keep putting one foot in front of the other.

And maybe that's what real motherhood is.
It's not just birthing you.
It's building you.

4
The '90s — Color, Chaos, and the Carpenter

If you ask any kid who survived the '90s, they'll probably tell you the same thing: it was the best fucking time to be alive.

The neon didn't just light up our shirts—it lit up our spirits. Lime green windbreakers. Hot pink slap bracelets. We weren't just wearing color—we were glowing in it. Our Disc-mans skipped if you looked at them sideways, but we carried them like holy relics. Super Nintendo. Sega Genesis. Mortal Kombat fatalities that made our jaws drop. Sonic tearing across the screen like he was late to everything—and we ran as fast as him home when the streetlights flickered on.

That was the rule: streetlights = time to go home.

You'd barrel through the door with grass-stained knees and fingers still sticky from freeze pops. If your mom wasn't on the landline, you might get a chance to log onto AOL. Dial-up internet was our baptism by fire—twenty minutes of praying no one picked up the phone. It wasn't just AOL, it was spiritual warfare against boredom. Well, for most of us, it was.

For others, time moved differently.

My cousin Emily wasn't caught up in the neon or the noise. She wasn't downloading AIM or trying to sneak into chatrooms. While the rest of us grew out of cartoons and into awkward adolescence, Emily stayed frozen in a toddler's innocence.

She had a mental handicap. I didn't have the words for it back then, but I knew what it meant. I could feel it in the way adults changed their voices around her—too sweet, too forced. I saw the way other kids stared too long or looked away too fast. The awkwardness. The discomfort. The cruelty that creeps in when people don't understand something.

I remember once, we were at a playground. Emily smiled at another girl, waving shyly, hoping to play. But the girl stared, turned away, whispered to her friends. Emily didn't understand, but I did. That protective fury I felt was new, heavy, and sharp. But Emily? She just kept smiling, oblivious to cruelty. I envied that innocence—and wanted to shield it forever.

Emily showed me early just how brutal the world can be to what it doesn't label as "normal." People fear what doesn't fit their version of the mold. And what they fear, they label.

But to me? Emily wasn't a label. She was love—pure, unfiltered, honest. She was soft edges in a world made of brick.

And while she stayed in that innocence, the rest of us were forced to grow up fast.

Beneath all the blinking lights and arcade tokens, something was shifting.

We were moving—from stability to survival.

From family dinners and new shoes to food stamps and WIC vouchers. From upper-middle-class routines to holding things together with whispered prayers and emotional patchwork. My family was beautiful but broken. Like stained glass, shattered across cobblestone.

Somewhere in the middle of that slow unraveling, my dad came into the picture. I was maybe four or five. Our bond began with weekends and movies. That was our ritual.

He'd pick me up from my mom's and take me to Aladdin's Castle—the arcade in the Sioux City mall. Ten bucks in quarters made me feel like royalty. After that, we'd grab popcorn and catch a movie I was probably way too young to watch.

I still remember standing up in the middle of The Lion King and yelling, "Oh my God, look at those elephants!" The whole theater laughed. My dad? Mortified. Me? Beaming.

One of my earliest memories with him. And one of my happiest.

But even that joy came with shadows.

At six years old, I didn't know how to say I felt guilty. I just knew when my dad's car pulled up, I hesitated at the door. Bobby's eyes, my little brother, watching me go he would be smiling, but quieter each time. I carried that quiet guilt like a weight shackled around my ankle, heavy but hidden, each weekend visit making it heavier.

How do you explain grief at that age? You don't. You just feel it. That tightness in your chest. The ache that whispers: I'm breaking something. I'm leaving him behind.

At my mom's house, life was tight. Strict. Evangelical. Four kids. One exhausted mom. The kind of faith where taking a piece of gum without asking might damn you forever.

At my dad's house? The Wild West.

R-rated movies. AC/DC blasting in the garage. Stepbrothers showing me anime that bent my brain sideways—Ninja Scroll, Tales from the Crypt, Freddy Krueger. I was eight. I was hooked.

I was somewhere between terrified and awakened. That house became a second home. And Diane—she became a second mother. Not a "step." Never a step. A soul. One who stayed up with me. Who made homemade noodles from scratch. Who gave me space to breathe when the world at home got too loud.

Meanwhile, the other side of my life was anchored by two of the greatest souls I've ever known—Leila and Fred Carlson. My great-grandparents.

Their home wasn't just a house. It was a gravitational force.

Everyone orbited through it. My uncle Fred lived in the basement. Aunt Ginnie upstairs. My grandma moving in and out like a satellite. But at the center of it all?

Fred Carlson.

Born September 4th, 1915. Son of Swedish immigrants. A carpenter. A giant. Six foot something. Built like a barn. Hands like lumber. Heart like velvet.

He built a house with his bare hands for my great grandmother and at that time, their four kids.

They moved in before the roof was even finished. Slept under plywood. Sandbags for insulation. Dreaming of a future they hadn't yet built—but they would.

That house still stands today. My brother lives there now.

But I'll never forget the day I saw the strongest man I knew—collapse.

It was a heart attack. In the backyard. He clutched his chest. Looked confused. The ambulance came. He survived—but something changed.

After that day, dementia moved in.

The man who once carved grandfather clocks from memory couldn't find the kitchen. The anchor began to drift. He cried. Often. Not because he was weak. But because somewhere deep down, he knew he was leaving—even if no one said it out loud.

And I felt it. Even as a kid, I felt it.

Because grief doesn't always come in black suits and funerals. Sometimes it sneaks in while the person is still breathing.

That decade—the '90s—it wasn't just fun and freeze pops.

It was full of that kind of grief.

My grandparent's marriage—unraveling. Addiction clawing through the cracks. Two people who couldn't love each other in the same room anymore.

But also… joy.

Cartoons. Arcades. Sleepovers. Popcorn at 2AM. Homemade noodles. A mom who stepped in to help. Another mom who never gave up. A carpenter who built more than homes—he built legacy.

After the heart attack, after the forgetting, after the tears of a man who once built kingdoms with wood and sweat—Fred was moved into care.

And no one really told me what that meant. They just said he'd be "safe."

But safe meant white walls and locked doors. Sterile hallways and plastic chairs. It meant seeing the man who once carried me on his shoulders now sitting in silence, staring through people he once held close.

And that's when the grief started—before the loss.

He was still alive. But he was already fading.

And I hated it.

I hated watching the house go quiet. The creaks didn't sound warm anymore. The air didn't smell like sawdust and pipe smoke. It smelled like waiting. Like absence. Like everyone was holding their breath.

My great-grandmother—Leila—a woman who had survived the Depression, raised seven kids, loved the same man for 60+ years—she broke. Quietly.

And the rest of us? We tried to pretend the center hadn't collapsed.

But it had.

The '90s didn't end with a bang. They faded quietly, slipping through my fingers, leaving only drifting echoes of laughter and loss.

Addiction. Separation. Financial collapse. Loneliness. Pain dressed in different costumes, but always showing up at the door.

And still… we laughed. We went to arcades. We yelled about elephants in movie theaters. We watched The Lion King and played Mortal Kombat and ran home when the streetlights flicked on.

Because somehow, we were still holding on.

The world had split in two—one half joy, one half grief. And I lived in both, learning how to smile with tears behind my eyes.

I didn't know it then, but the '90s weren't just my childhood. They were my education in grief. Not the kind that shows up dressed in a suit, but the kind that creeps in when you don't need a casket. The kind that makes a six-year-old feel guilty for having a dad when his brother doesn't. The kind that whispers— even giants fall.

And yet, I wouldn't trade it.

Because even in the chaos, they gave me roots. They gave me stories. They gave me the first blueprint of what it looks like to keep showing up when life doesn't get easier.

They gave me a map for the storm I didn't know was coming.

5

Fred & Leila Carlson

The first-time death actually hit me—the way it claws into your soul and makes you feel something irreversible—wasn't when my Uncle Jeff died.

Jeff's death felt distant, like a shadow behind glass—something tragic but unreachable. But Fred's death? It was raw, immediate, and real. It reached through my chest and tore open a wound I didn't know I had.

I mean, yeah, I knew he'd been killed. I knew he'd been murdered. Shot with a fucking gun. But I never met him, not that I can remember anyway. So, it never really landed. It was just a headline in my family's history. A fact. Not a feeling.

But by the late '90s, as everything that once held our world together started to fray… that's when death got loud.

It was 1998. Columbine.

I was ten. I remember the TV showing kids pouring out of their school like ants fleeing a burning anthill. News anchors hovered like vultures. Kids sobbing, screaming, "They're killing them! They're killing them!" And I remember thinking—wait… killing? In school? That's not supposed to happen. School was for spelling tests and snow days. Not murder. Not blood on linoleum.

It was the first time I saw death on a screen and understood that those kids weren't going home. That their parents were about to walk into the worst kind of silence. The kind you never come back from. Churches started talking about it. Prayers were being said. And for the first time, I realized the world could be violent in a way you don't get to turn off.

Then came 1999. The fear of Y2K. People were losing their shit thinking computers were going to implode, planes would fall from the sky, and we'd all be living in Mad Max territory by sunrise. We had one of those clunky Gateway computers with the cow-print box—back when your tech looked like it came straight off a dairy farm in Iowa. I remember staring at that thing on New Year's Eve, wondering if it would explode at midnight like everyone said it would. Y2K panic was everywhere, and I was just a kid waiting for the digital world to combust.

What made that computer even more special was how we got it. My grandma worked at a Gateway call center warehouse in South Dakota. The pay wasn't great, but it was enough to get her a discount on a new computer. And when she got that new one, she passed the old one down to us. We couldn't have afforded one otherwise. If it wasn't for her, we wouldn't have had one at all. That was her way. She didn't have much, but what she had, she gave.

She lived in this little two-bedroom apartment in Sioux Falls— modest, worn, always warm. Somehow, on Christmas, she could cram all of us into that tiny space like we were stuffing a suitcase that wouldn't zip. My aunt Kim, Emily, my mom, all four of us kids—stacked on couches, floors, whatever spot you could find. Cramped, chaotic, loud. But together. Held by chewed gum and hope. That's what love looked like in our family. And soon, that love was about to be tested in the deepest, cruelest way.

My great-grandpa Fred—the strongest man I ever knew—was fading.

The evangelical part of my family treated death like a spiritual checkpoint. It wasn't about pain. It was about "the journey." About heaven and peace and singing someone home. But I was eleven. And none of that shit made it easier.

I hadn't seen my great grandpa in months. And when I finally did, on November 3, 1999, I barely recognized him. He was just skin wrapped in plastic over bone. A shell of the man I used to sit on like a throne. The man who could carry a child on one shoulder and a lumber beam on the other. The man who built the house that held four generations. Now, he was slipping into shadow.

We prayed. We watched. We waited. It felt more like a seance than a goodbye. Not a moment of closure, but a slow unraveling of something sacred.

And then came November 5th.

I was at his bedside. My grandma sat on my left, Uncle Rick on my right, Uncle Fred behind me. My mom and my grandma's sisters were nearby, their presence a blur through the veil of that moment. My grandma took his hand—the same hand that used to build homes and hold grandkids like feathers—and placed it in mine. He was so small.

I felt his pulse faint beneath thin, paper-like skin, his fingertips cold against mine. The sound of quiet crying and whispered prayers blurred together around us, and I remember how small he felt, how impossibly fragile. This man who once carried worlds was now weightless, slipping quietly from my grasp.

She leaned in and whispered, "You can tell him you love him. He can hear you."

His eyes fluttered open, just barely. And I told him, "I love you so much."

He smiled. Took in one last, deep breath. His chest rose.

And when it fell—it didn't rise again.

Just like that, he was gone. I held my great-grandpa's hand as he died.

There was no thunderclap. No music. No big cinematic clarity. Just finality. Just air that suddenly felt thinner. Just the weight of absence filling the room like smoke. Tears erupted. My grandma broke first. Then my mom. Then me. The air changed. The king of our family was gone.

And Leila… she broke next.

My great-grandmother—this elegant, fire-and-honey woman of faith—started to fade almost instantly. They always said it was a broken heart. And if you ask me, they were right.

She was deeply religious. The kind of woman who thought sarcasm might be a sin. But she could also laugh so hard the sound would bounce off the walls and stay there. She was grace and grit wrapped in a cardigan. A woman who raised seven kids in the house her husband built from nothing. Slept under halfway built roof on top of bags of concrete until that home had walls. Loved Fred for most of her life. And without him, she began to unravel.

Leila once held the family together with smiles, strong coffee, and stubborn faith. She would hum old hymns softly while washing dishes, melodies rising above the chaos of our family gatherings. Seeing that same vibrant woman now silent, eyes distant, felt unnatural—like watching warmth leave the sun.

December came, and Christmas felt like a funeral. January followed, and we all pretended the New Year meant something. I turned twelve that month. The year I'd survive Y2K and join the elite club of preteens who now got to call themselves "teenagers-in-waiting." That mattered to me, for some reason. But all the excitement vanished before it even started. The day came and went, and so did the feeling.

Y2K didn't bring the apocalypse. No aliens. No chaos. Just another year. But the world still came to a crashing haunt. At least, ours did.

On March 26, 2000, we gathered in the living room.

The same living room Fred Carlson built. The same room that had held birthdays and board games, roast dinners and loud, holy arguments. The room that used to hum with life.

We surrounded her in her living room —every one of us. But unlike Fred, she waited until no one was looking.

She waited until laughter faded into quiet conversation, until eyes drifted elsewhere, until the weight of attention eased from her shoulders. And only then—when no one was watching, when no one would carry the burden of witnessing—did she slip quietly into the next world, leaving behind nothing but peace.

We think—no, we know—she did it that way on purpose. She didn't want to be watched. Didn't want anyone to bear the weight of her leaving. She didn't want her final breath to be a burden, so when the room went quiet and no one was watching, she slipped away.

Leila Carlson died in the home her husband built for her. A home where she raised babies and buried love and grew old with dignity.

And just like that, the heart of our family stopped beating. The silence that followed wasn't just quiet—it was deafening, echoing through every empty room, every holiday gathering, every heartbeat that now carried grief.

6

The Summer Pulse

So yeah— that fucking sucked.

When you're twelve years old, and the goddamn Thor of your multiverse falls—and you're the one holding his hand as he goes down—how the hell are you supposed to make sense of that? You can't. But somehow, you just do. You have to. There's no instruction manual. No magic prayer. No adult in the room who truly knows what to say. The heartbeat of the family stops, and all that's left is this ringing silence—and in that silence, if you're lucky, you search for a pulse.

And I found one.

While my grandma, her brothers and sisters, and the generations around them did their best to carry the unbearable loss, grieving in fragments and in silence, I was just a kid standing in the wreckage of what was left. I was feeling all of it, absorbing the weight of a legacy that had collapsed, and still being told I was probably too young to understand. Like the religious narratives were enough to explain death, to define grief, to comfort the fucking crater that had just opened in my chest.

But I didn't need a sermon. I needed a hand. And even though my dad was in jail at the time, and even though that entire year felt like a back-and-forth tidal wave of chaos, I still had a heartbeat nearby. Diane.

She never disappeared. Not even with my dad behind bars. She stayed close—not in theory, but in reality. I still went to her house on the weekends, just to be with her. Not him. Just her.

Looking back, that summer might've been what saved me.

Her house was alive. She had four kids—my two stepbrothers and two stepsisters—all older, most with kids of their own. Which technically made me, at twelve years old, a step-uncle. Wild, right? I was only a few years older than the kids I was "uncle" to. It felt both hilarious and strangely grounding. That summer, Diane wasn't just being Grandma—she was in full-on mom mode again, raising her grandkids Derek and Joslyn. Two little fireballs who filled that house with noise and laughter, the kind of chaos that reminded you life was still beating.

And I loved those kids. Deeply. In a way that surprised me. But what surprised me more was how my dad lit up around them. He adored Derek and Joslyn—and if I'm being honest, sometimes it felt like more than he loved me. He seemed more confident around them. More at ease. More patient. It stung in a quiet, complicated way like when a bruise is forming under the skin, invisible but constantly aching. How could I compete with innocence that didn't carry his guilt? I didn't resent them; I loved them. But the unfairness gnawed at me silently, shaping the questions about worth and love I'd carry for years.

But none of that mattered when I was there. Because what really mattered—what grounded me— was her.

Diane would take me rummaging every weekend, like clockwork. We'd stay up late—sometimes until one, two in the morning—talking, laughing, sharing stories, listening to the hum of the night. She taught me how to cook, how to do laundry, how to fold clothes properly, and most importantly, how to talk. Really talk. And damn, did she love to talk.

She asked questions like it was her gift. What did I remember about Grandpa? What made me smile about Grandma Leila? What felt unfair? What didn't make sense? She didn't push. She didn't pretend to have all the answers. She just kept opening the door, over and over, encouraging me to walk through it in my own time.

I remember sitting in the kitchen late at night with her, feeling guilty for questioning things I'd always been told were certain. 'What if none of this is true?' I whispered, afraid even to say it. Diane paused, took a sip of her tea, and said softly, 'Then maybe our job isn't to have all the answers. Maybe it's just to ask the questions.' Which honestly, I remember, it felt like breathing after holding my breath my whole life.

We'd be up by eight the next morning, no matter how late we stayed up, and hit the garage sale circuit like we were on a mission. Diane would have the newspaper spread out across her bed cross legged, garage sale ads circled in pen, routes mapped out like a general prepping for war. She was strategic—hit the good neighborhoods first, the listings with big promises. She taught me to look for value, to dig through junk with curiosity, to never overlook something that just needed a little love.

I was always allowed to pick out something small. A toy, a trinket—whatever caught my eye. But there was a catch: I wasn't allowed to just grab it and go. If it cost fifty cents, I had to try to talk it down to a quarter. If it was a quarter, I had to shoot for a dime. And if I didn't try, I didn't get it. I hated that rule at first. But eventually, I got it.

She wasn't just teaching me how to bargain. She was teaching me how to use my voice. How to speak up. How to ask for what I wanted, even if it made me uncomfortable. Even if it was just over a toy car or a worn-out action figure. It wasn't about the price. It was about the power of connection.

We spent those rides talking. About her childhood, her siblings—all seven or eight of them, a full-blown army of personalities—and about the past. I met some of them later at a big family reunion. I felt like an outsider at first, standing in a sea of people I didn't recognize. But Diane made sure I didn't feel outside for long. She pulled me in, grounded me, reminded me that I belonged—not just because she said it, but because she showed it.

She didn't treat me like a stepson. She looked at me like I was hers. And that's exactly how she made me feel.

That summer, she brought laughter back into my life. She reminded me how to breathe again. How to feel joy without guilt. How to talk through the wreckage and find something beautiful in the ruins. Her house, her energy, her presence—it was always moving. Always alive. She was one of those people who operated at a million miles an hour. Always caffeinated. Always in motion. She had a white Chrysler convertible that year—a total piece of shit, looking back—but at the time, it was a chariot.

We'd cruise around town with the top down, Z98 Rock blasting, wind in our faces. She'd glance over and shout, "In four years, you'll be sixteen. This car'll be yours." I believed her. Why wouldn't I? Even the things she said casually felt like promises to a kid who desperately needed stability.

When I started to question everything to believe, Diane didn't shut me down. She didn't preach. She asked questions. She let me wonder out loud. She gave me space to wrestle with the pain of watching our faith fall apart while our family fell apart too. She let me say, "This doesn't make sense." Because it didn't.

But she made sense. She was doing the thing our faith claimed to do: showing up.

She hugged me every time she saw me. Long, grounding, wordless hugs. And now? I'm a hugger. I hug my friends. I hug coworkers. I hug when I say hello and hug when I say goodbye. Because I'm not just hugging you—I'm saying something. That came from her.

Her hugs said, "Even if I'm leaving, I'm still with you." And that summer—that fucked-up, beautiful, healing summer—it was great. I was twelve. Still grieving. Still piecing together what the hell life was. But I had someone who kept asking questions, who kept showing up, who kept helping me relive the best parts of the people I lost, not just the day I lost them.

Because that's the whole point, isn't it? It's about how they lived—not just when they died.

And I wish I could say, "And from then on, I lived happily ever after." But life's not a movie, and this book sure as hell isn't a fairy tale.

My dad got out of jail. I saw him a few times toward the end of the year. Then something happened—I don't remember what, exactly—but I was pulled away again. No Christmas with them. Just my mom. No more weekends around Diane.

The gap widened. I hadn't talked to her in a while. And I missed her.

Then came my thirteenth birthday.

It was a big deal. I'd been counting down the days, the hours, the seconds. After years of chaos and heartbreak, I was ready to level up. Becoming a teenager felt like becoming a goddamn superhero.

That day, I came home from a youth group church retreat and saw my grandpa sitting at the dining room table, still covered in drywall mud and plaster. He looked like he'd just fought a house—and won.

"Danny-boy!" he called out, grinning. "Got a surprise for your birthday downstairs."

My eyes lit up. No way. There was no chance he finished a section of the basement—not with the money we didn't have, and definitely not with our landlord. But I bolted to the basement, rounded the corner, stepped through an open door…

And froze.

There it was. My own fucking room.

The smell of fresh carpet glue and wood still lingered in the air. I ran my fingers along the smooth drywall, the perfectly taped seams, and felt a lump form in my throat. It wasn't just a room but a promise. A sanctuary. A piece of himself he'd given me, something tangible and real to hold onto when everything else felt slippery.

He had built me a space, with his own two hands, from nothing. No more sharing with my brothers. No more noise. For the first time in my life, I had space. My own space. A place to breathe. To be alone. To grow.

When I came back upstairs, still stunned, my grandpa wiped his hands, smiled, and said he'd knocked it out in under two days. Just like that. No big deal.

But it was a big deal. One of the biggest.

I hugged him like I never wanted to let go—and he hugged me back, even tighter. Looking back, I think that moment meant just as much to him as it did to me.

And as wild as that was… more surprises were coming.

My mom, who didn't always get a lot of one-on-one time with us, surprised me next.

"Just you and me tonight," she said.

She took me to King Sea—the Chinese spot with the legendary crab legs. We laughed. We ate. I ordered something too spicy and immediately regretted it. She gave me hell for it, and I gave it right back. Funny now, since I always joke about how she thinks salt is spicy.

Then we pulled into the driveway. It was dark. Quiet. I opened the door.

Boom.

Lights on. Room packed. Friends from school. Friends from church. Family. Everyone.

A surprise party.

I froze, heart slamming into my sternum. The smell of birthday cake and cheap pizza filled the air. Someone's cologne was too strong. People erupted in laughter and cheers, a wall of noise wrapping around me. My face flushed hot, my pulse racing— joy, shock, disbelief. It was overwhelming. It was perfect.

And in that moment—surrounded by noise, chaos, joy—I felt something shift. I felt hope.

And then… it got better.

Diane showed up.

My dad stayed in the car, but she came to the porch, handed me a gift, gave me a hug, and said,
"Happy birthday. Welcome to being a teenager. I know how much you've been waiting for this."

Seeing Diane standing there, breath visible in the winter air, felt like oxygen after being underwater too long. Her hug was tight, fierce, the kind that makes your heart hurt in the best way possible. It said everything words couldn't, that even when life pulled us apart, we found our way back. She made promises with her presence alone, and right then, I believed them all.

And that moment—that fucking moment—gave me everything I needed.

I had spent so long aching for connection. Watching people slip through my fingers. But that night, I stood in a room full of people who chose to show up. I had a hug from Diane. A meal

with my mom. A room from my grandpa. And a moment—
finally—for me.

I went to bed that night in my own room. My own little world.
Full of love. Full of chaos. Full of possibility.

I was thirteen.

And I was about to fucking dominate the world.

7

The Year of Forgotten Healing

Before we dive into the rest—the chaos, the heartbreak, the teenage years that weren't anything like I imagined—I need to stop here. This is the pause. The breath before the plunge. Because looking back now, it's fucking wild how much you can learn from a single year. And it's even crazier how you don't realize the impact of that year until decades later, when the dust settles and you're standing in the life you built from the rubble.

When I was twelve, I thought I'd already lived through the worst. I thought losing my great grandparents was as deep as grief could go. I thought turning thirteen meant leveling up— becoming a teenager, becoming stronger, smarter, untouchable. What I didn't know was that pain has its own schedule, and joy, healing, and heartbreak often come tangled together. But that year—the year I was twelve—that was the year that gave me something rare.

It gave me stability.
It gave me predictability.
It gave me Diane.

Looking back now, I realize one of the most important things Diane gave me wasn't just love or attention—it was consistency. She was fucking there. When everything else in my life felt like shifting sand, she was the steady place I could stand. Not once. Not occasionally. Every single time.

And science backs this up—though I didn't know that shit at twelve. I just knew I could count on her.

Studies show that predictability in childhood is one of the most essential ingredients for emotional security. It reduces stress, anxiety, and fear. When a kid knows what to expect, their brain stops fighting to survive and starts learning how to live. It creates space to explore, think, ask questions, and feel—without that constant background hum of fear.

Predictability doesn't sound sexy, and no one goes out to get a leadership book titled 'How to Be Boring as Hell.' But damn, boring was exactly what I needed, and exactly what Diane delivered, one comforting, predictable garage sale at a time.

That was Diane.

While the adults in my life were grieving, stretched thin, or just surviving, Diane created order in the storm. She gave me a rhythm. Friday nights at her house. Late-night talks. Rummage sales every Saturday morning. Teaching me to cook. Letting me talk through my pain without ever trying to slap a religious Band-Aid over it. She didn't try to fix me. She just sat with me.

That kind of stability? That shit matters. Big time.

There's research that shows kids who experience consistent caregiving—where routines are stable and emotional reactions are predictable—develop better executive functioning, stronger memory retention, and healthier attachments. It literally wires the brain for safety, connection, and problem-solving.

I didn't know it then, but she was shaping how I would handle life later—how I would think through hard situations, how I'd lead people, how I'd show up in the world. She didn't preach. She asked questions. And when I started pushing back on the evangelical faith I was raised in at my other house—when I questioned where God was during all this pain—she didn't shut me down. She got curious. That curiosity gave me permission to be myself, to think out loud, to process things in my own fucked-up, searching kind of way. And damn, that's healing. Not being told what to think but being invited to think.

She also taught me the power of memory—how talking about people keeps them alive. How sharing their stories, their quirks, their weird sayings and beautiful flaws keeps them close. That's not some spiritual fluff, either—that's neuroscience. The more we reflect on someone with warmth and detail, the stronger the neural connections become. We keep them tethered to us, not through sorrow, but through connection.

She'd ask about Grandpa Fred's laugh—how it sounded echoing through the house he built. How did everyone react to him? She'd ask me to describe Grandma Leila's gentle voice, the way she hummed softly while folding laundry, or while she cooked one of her famous home cooked meals. Every story Diane asked me to share wasn't just nostalgia—it was a heartbeat, a living connection to people I loved. She showed me memory isn't just recalling someone—it's keeping them alive inside us.

Diane did that. And she did it naturally.

She taught me how to talk, how to laugh again, how to keep breathing without guilt. She moved at a million miles an hour, was always caffeinated, always moving, blasting rock in a white Chrysler convertible that, to me, it looked like freedom.

And she gave me freedom.
To question.
To feel.
To exist without shame.

I didn't know it then, but all of this—all that predictability—was becoming the foundation for the man I'd become later. When I got older, when I stepped into leadership roles, when I had teams looking to me for guidance, I realized that same rhythm Diane gave me—that same stability—that was what I brought into every room I walked into.

Predictability became one of the greatest tools in my leadership toolbox.

People don't need a perfect leader—they need a steady one. Someone they can count on to show up, to ask questions, to actually fucking listen. Someone who doesn't make them flinch. Diane showed me that before I even knew what the word leadership meant. She modeled what it looked like to guide without control, to support without smothering, to hold space without forcing a fix.

And I carried that forward. Into work. Into friendships. Into adulthood. Into coaching and development. Into every team I've ever led. I became a leader who believes in structure, in clarity, in showing up the same way every day—because that's what people need when they're overwhelmed, when they're grieving, when they're trying to grow through something they don't even have language for yet.

That came from my mom, Diane.

And even though I didn't know it at the time, that year should have set the foundation. It should have been the start of everything stable, everything I needed to keep moving forward when life got dark again. But the truth is, foundations only work if they're reinforced.

No one warned me that the walls Diane built around me—walls of safety, laughter, and steadiness—would soon shake violently, cracks forming faster than I could patch them. The comfort she gave me was real, but the storm coming was stronger. I didn't see it yet, but somewhere on the horizon, darkness was building again, preparing to test every lesson, every hug, every fragile piece of hope she had given me.

Because in 2001, I turned thirteen. And everything I thought I understood about stability, love, and loss was about to get fucking destroyed.

8

Plans Fall Apart

It had only been two months since my thirteenth birthday and just shy of a year since my great grandma passed. That strange, haunting milestone where the world reminds you of your losses whether you're ready or not. This is the point in the story where you learn how people react, respond, and say the wildest shit when death is involved. Because death? It messes with the human mind. And when it's someone close? Fucking forget it.

Psychologists call it "cognitive dissonance." The brain doesn't know how to hold two truths at once—grief and normalcy, celebration and collapse. It short-circuits. That's why people say the wrong things, snap without warning, or fall completely silent. Loss disrupts the map of how we think the world is supposed to work.

It was May 16, 2001. A Friday. Sixth grade was wrapping up, and I was looking forward to a weekend with Dylan—my best friend through all of elementary school. By the time middle school hit, we'd been split. He went to Hoover, the new, shiny, up-to-date school. I went to Woodrow Wilson—literally the castle on the hill in Sioux City, Iowa. A building so old it came with legends: cockroaches the size of mice, bathrooms that whispered secrets, lockers that refused to open unless you begged. Hoover was "preppy." Woodrow was "ghetto." Middle school drama and rivalry. The cockroaches, for the record, were normal-sized.

Despite being in different schools, Dylan and I stayed close. Phone calls whenever our parents let us. Sleepovers when we could. He was the loud, popular extrovert, and I was the broke, guarded introvert. But he never judged. We were opposites, and it worked. That Thursday, we'd made a master plan—get our parents to approve not just one night, but two. A weekend sleepover. The kind of scheme only teenage boys could dream up. I was locked in, fully ready with my pitch. After that, I'd call Dylan, pretend my mom was about to drive me over, then hustle over there on foot. We didn't have a car, but it was only about a mile and a half, maybe two, and I knew the shortcuts like the back of my hand.

I walked in the front door of our house on 26th Street and immediately knew something was off. Empty. Dead quiet. Which was weird, because one of my mom's main sources of income was running an in-home daycare. There were always toddlers crawling around, kids throwing toys, somebody crying. Add in my younger brothers and their friends, and it was a madhouse. You had to be fast, loud, and clever just to get noticed. But now? No sound. No chaos. Just stillness.

I figured my brothers were around somewhere. Their backpacks were by the door. Shoes scattered. Probably out back or running around the block. As I turned to head outside and find them, the silence broke. My brother burst out of our next-door neighbor's house—Shirley and Ted's place. They were in their late 60s, maybe 70s. Faithful, kind, deeply rooted in their beliefs. My mom and Shirley bonded over Bible verses and spiritual rabbit holes. They fed each other's curiosity and love for scripture.

"Where's Mom?!" I hollered across the two yards.

"In there with Shirley," Josh yelled back, pointing over his shoulder. "She's sad. I'm going to find JJ!"

That wasn't part of the plan. Why was she sad? Where were the daycare kids?

I walked across both yards and up to Shirley's front door. Light knock on the screen. "Come in, Danny," she said gently.

Inside, my mom was sitting at the table with her back to me, Shirley at the head of the table. They were holding hands. Praying. Kleenex box to the side. I knew that pose. I knew those tears.

I jumped into my pitch anyway.

"Mom, I haven't seen Dylan in forever, and well, here's the deal—"

"Not now, Daniel, we need to talk," she interrupted.

"Okay, but real quick—just hear me out. I haven't seen Dylan in forever and I haven't seen Dad or Diane either. Not since my birthday. Or even talked to them. And Dylan—"

Her voice cut through mine like static.

"Danny, please stop. You're not going to Dylan's. The answer is no—"

"Hold on, hold on, before you jump to no, just hear me out—"

"Diane died, Daniel. You're not going to Dylan's."

Her words slammed into my chest like a car crash. They didn't sound real. They didn't even register as words at first. Just white noise.

"What do you mean? What? How? When?! WHAT?!" My voice cracked, splintered, spiraled.

I stumbled out onto the porch, heart hammering, limbs suddenly heavy as if filled with sand. My chest felt crushed, every breath was painful, shallow, impossible. I sat down hard, holding myself together, but my body betrayed me—shaking uncontrollably, sobs breaking free despite my efforts to contain them. Diane was dead, and my body understood it before my mind could.

I sat on the porch, choking on the air. I didn't know how to breathe. The pulse I had found—the rhythm I'd built since my great-grandfather's death—was gone.

This is where time usually stops for people. For me, it skipped. That day, I went from being excited about a weekend sleepover to becoming a grown adult in a thirteen-year-old's body. I entered survivor mode. It wasn't a choice. It was instinct.

Research shows that children who experience early trauma— especially the death of a caregiver or someone central to their emotional security—often shift into hyper-vigilance and maturity far beyond their years. They begin reading the room like a chessboard, anticipating emotions, managing others' reactions, protecting themselves through control. It's not development—it's defense. It's armor.

In an instant, I understood I was on my own. No one else would step in to guide me through this. Diane had been my anchor, and now she was gone. I was forced to be my own protector, my own voice of reason, my own comfort. At thirteen, I stood there, feeling decades older, hollowed out by loss.

The air around me thickened, like breathing through water. Diane couldn't be dead. Not Diane, who'd always been there, who had always been my compass in the storm. My mind scrambled for proof she was still here—her laugh, her voice— but everything was silent. It was like the whole universe had stopped speaking the language I knew.

Diane had taught me so much. But now she was gone. My grandfather's vices had finally taken hold. He was in jail. Not for anything monstrous but from drugs. But it was enough to make sure he wasn't there. My dad hadn't been around in over a year. And I knew this wouldn't be the thing to bring him back.

I was thirteen on the outside. But inside? I was already navigating the world like an adult— reading people's tones, analyzing facial expressions, predicting what version of someone I'd get that day so I could stay safe. I walked back inside and drifted to my room—the one my grandpa built me for my birthday. The one that had once felt like hope.

Now, it felt like a cave.

It was supposed to be a place of safety, but it became my isolation chamber. I pulled back. Learned to keep my voice small. I cried in silence. I processed in corners. And I memorized the new map of my life: who was gone, who was silent, and who I had left to lean on.

No one sat me down gently. No one explained. No one wrapped me in arms and said, "It's okay to fall apart." My introduction to this kind of grief was loud, then abruptly quiet. I was sobbing one minute, and alone the next.

Diane was gone. And with her, a part of me went quiet too.

9

Buried Without a Funeral

Diane was fucking gone.

It was finite. Carved into reality like stone. There was no twist in the universe that could undo it, no prayer strong enough to rewind time. She was forty-four. Her heart just stopped. That's it. No warning. No explanation. Just a silence so loud it rang through my bones like a church bell. Echoing. Unrelenting. Crushing.

In the nights leading up to her funeral, I cried like the world owed me an answer—but none came. I cried to God. I cried to the stars. I cried into a pillow until it was soaked through, heavy with snot and heartbreak. But nothing talked back. Not God. Not the stars. Not even the fucking walls. No divine whisper. No clarity. Just silence. And the impossible ache of knowing that the one person who saw me, who held space for me, who made me feel like I mattered, had been ripped away without a trace of justice. Just… gone.

And then came the funeral.

As emotionally charged as you'd expect—and worse. Diane's husband—my dad—sat in the front row, drunk. Swollen with grief and guilt and years of regret. He looked like a crumbling mountain, hunched over in a button-down shirt that didn't quite fit right, breathing like he was holding the sky on his back. The room behind him was packed. Every chair filled, every aisle lined with people standing, sobbing. The air itself felt wet with grief. Thick. Heavy. There was music playing, but the sobbing swallowed the sound. You couldn't make out the lyrics—just the dull rhythm of loss in the background.

Then the pastor stood up.

And my dad's eyes locked in like a target had just been painted on that man's chest.

My dad's a big motherfucker. Towering. Broad. And next to me—a chubby, emotionally confused and distraught thirteen-year-old—he looked like the final boss in a game I never signed up to play. Not chiseled like a bodybuilder. He had the kind of strength you get from slinging bags of concrete mix and hauling rebar. Concrete foreman strong. Calloused. Raw. Survival forged into skin and bone.

I used to tell him he sounded like the Terminator without the accent. He'd laugh, take a long drag from his cigarette, and say Schwarzenegger couldn't last one day in his boots. "Pretty boy stage muscles ain't got shit on hard-earned concrete strength." That was my dad. And that day, he wasn't aiming at machines—he was aiming at God.

The pastor cleared his throat, trying to gently reel the room back into something resembling grace.

"God loves all His children…"
"HA!" my dad barked, loud enough to make every neck turn.

"While we may not understand why He takes those we love so soon…"

"That's fucking rich," he growled.

The tension shifted in an instant. You could feel it crawling through the room. People adjusting in their seats. Eyes flicking between the pastor and my dad. I kept my head down. Eyes fixed on the carpet. The threads began to blur and twist under my gaze as I tried to disappear into the floor. I wasn't just embarrassed—I was in awe. This wasn't just my father. This was a man unraveling. Live. In front of everyone.

The death of a spouse is one of the most traumatic events a human being can endure. It increases the risk of depression, substance abuse, and early death. The widowhood effect is real—within the first three months of losing a partner, the surviving spouse's risk of death increases by up to 66%. Grief doesn't just break your heart—it rewires your body. It sinks its claws into your bones and slowly unravels your ability to hold yourself together.

And my dad was coming apart at the seams. His breath was labored. His pain slurred and sharp. The liquor on him hit me from a foot away—this thick, acidic cloud that reeked of cheap whiskey and desperation. I remember thinking, so this is what hell smells like.

"You have got to be fucking kidding me!" he shouted.

And honestly—who could blame him?

How do you ask a man to sit quietly while they eulogize the woman he loved—the woman he lost to a goddamn heart attack—without him ever getting the chance to make it right? How do you expect him to fold his hands, and whisper amens while a stranger tries to explain away her death with platitudes and scripture? Even at thirteen, I got it. This wasn't just a man losing his wife. This was a man being swallowed whole by every mistake he never fixed, every chance he didn't take.

And me?

I wanted to scream with him.

I wanted to flip every fucking pew and set the place on fire and scream at every smiling face that thought they knew who she was, what she meant, how this should feel. I wanted to crack the world open with the same kind of rage burning in his eyes.
But I was thirteen.

Too old to be a kid.

Too young to fall apart in public.

So, I kept my head down. Let my eyes burn. And when the heat got too much, I closed them— because maybe if I couldn't see them, they couldn't see me.

After the funeral, we went back to her house. Her kitchen. Her couch. Her air. The place where we used to stay up late watching movies. Where she taught me to cook, to ask questions, to breathe when the grief tried to suffocate me. I sat on the couch— the same spot she used to nap, laugh, talk. I tried to live in the memories like she taught me. But it was impossible. Her absence screamed over every memory I reached for. And the noise in the house—the strangers, the crying, the yelling, the crashing of people who didn't know how to grieve without throwing something—it drowned out everything else. It felt like I was underwater. Watching the room through glass. Screaming without sound.

Her family—my stepfamily—was unraveling too. The kids she helped raise were being sent to homes they weren't ready for.

Her siblings were trying to stay upright while grief kicked out their knees. My older step-siblings, who hated my dad with reason I understood, barely looked at me. And when they did? It was like I was him.

I wasn't Diane's stepson anymore. I wasn't family. I was the extension of the wrecking ball they blamed for the whole collapse.

So, I kept quiet. Faded into the edges.

And then my aunt called me over.

"Hey Danny Joe, come over here real quick."

I hated that name. Hated it. It sounded like the punchline to a cruel joke. Like I belonged on the shelf next to a gas station lottery ticket and a bottle of Mountain Dew. Diane used to tease me about it, make it a joke, spin it into something sweet. But when it came from my aunt, it didn't feel like a joke. It felt like a boundary. Like a line drawn in Sharpie.

"This is Bobby's kid."

Not Daniel. Not Danny. Not even just "my nephew." Just Bobby's kid. Labeled. Boxed. Branded.

That night, I discarded Danny, Danny Joe, and every childhood nickname, burying him with everything else I'd lost. Dan wasn't just a new name—it was armor. Something stronger, colder, sharper. But hidden deep inside it was the warmth of her voice. Diane's voice. The only echo of comfort I had left.

I've only told one person this—that I chose that name not just because I wanted something stronger, but because it sounded like Diane. That every time someone said it, it felt like I was keeping a part of her close. Her name lived in mine.

That night, I wasn't a son. I wasn't a stepson or a brother. I wasn't even a person.

I was just… there.

Later, Jasmine—one of my stepsisters—sat beside me. The alcohol was strong on her breath. She kissed my forehead and whispered, "You'll always be my little brother. No matter what." Then she stood up and walked away.

I never saw her again. Or JaNon. Or Terry. Or Eli.

A whole branch of my life, cut off without warning.

Just silence.

And what I didn't realize until much later was—it had already happened before. After that summer, I never saw Derek or Joslyn again either. Not until we were all grown. They disappeared just as suddenly. One moment we were playing in the hallway, laughing, and the next? Gone. No explanation. Just another room gone dark.

I didn't know then that I was already grieving families before I even figured out who I was.

After sitting alone on the couch for what felt like hours, the house eventually emptied. My dad didn't say much. Just one line.

"Love you. Goin' bed. Night."

And that was it.

This was the part where Diane's voice should've kicked in. Speak up. Use your voice. Keep them alive by talking. But how do you speak when no one wants to hear? When is every attempt met with silence or slammed doors? I tried. And I failed. I had the tools—but no strength to wield them.

A few weeks later, my dad made a final attempt. Said he'd pick me up after school. Four o'clock. He showed up four and a half hours late. Drunk. Again. I got in the car because I didn't know what else to do. His house was dark, cold, reeking of smoke and rot. The floors were sticky. The air felt stale. He handed me a blanket and passed out. I left the next day by early afternoon.

Trauma doesn't come with instructions. You can't step into Tony Stark's Iron Man suit and expect it to work. That thing's built from memory, precision, legacy, pain, and fire. Without training, it'll crush you.

Diane gave me the blueprint. But I wasn't ready for the weight.

I didn't know how to pause. How to feel and still move. How to breathe through the pain. I didn't know how to grieve out loud.

All I knew was survival.

And then—barely into the start of 7th grade—September 11th, 2001.

I was in Ms. Roe's English class when someone came in whispering. She turned on the TV mounted in the corner—the same one we used for Bill Nye—but this time, nobody laughed. One of the twin towers was already burning. Then we watched the second plane hit. Live.

No one spoke. Some of us didn't even know what the Twin Towers were. But we knew enough to be afraid. Teachers cried. Kids asked if war was coming. And I sat there, watching it all, thinking about my Uncle Jeff. How he died on duty. Shot while guarding his post in Hawaii. How my family never recovered.

And in that silence, something rooted itself in me.

I didn't know how, or when, or why—but I knew I would serve.

By November, the weather shifted again—sunny, weirdly warm. Almost a year to the day since I'd broken my wrist falling off the garage roof. Back then, it was for a snowball war. This year, I had a new hustle.

The Shopper.

Wednesday ad paper route. Two hours of work for a hundred bucks. I was ballin'. That day, I loaded up, slung the bag over my shoulder, hopped on my bike, and started my route. Wind in my face. Plans with Dylan waiting after.

I didn't make it five blocks.

The strap slipped into my spokes turning me into an astronaut preparing to break Earth's gravity.

Then I launched. I raced towards space making it three feet into the air before gravity regained the upper hand.

My body slammed into the pavement, bones cracking like dry branches underfoot, pain radiating in white-hot pulses that stole every bit of air from my lungs. Gravel scraped raw lines across my skin, each breath like knives slicing through my chest.

I just managed to choke out my landline number to a stranger. And my mom showed up.

"Do you need an ambulance?" someone asked.

'He's fine,' she said, and the cold dismissal in her voice stung worse than the pulverized bones in my leg. Diane would've knelt beside me, brushed my hair back, whispered strength into my pain. But Diane wasn't here. And my mother's voice made that absence feel even more brutal.

Even through the agony, I thought: Diane would never fucking say that.

Eventually, we got to the ER. The X-ray lit up- it's light revealing what looked more like snapped tree branches than bone. My tibia, fibula, ankle obliterated. The doctor said, "It's bad." My mom just stared. I didn't say anything.

Because I didn't need to.

She didn't listen.
Diane would've.

That night, after the procedure, my mom went home.

I woke up alone.

In the dark hospital room, the silence settled over me like a heavy, damp blanket. The hum of the machines blended with my pulse, each beep marking time I couldn't measure anymore. I stared into the shadows, feeling Diane's absence like a ghost beside me, her voice drowned by the sterile emptiness around me.

And that's when it hit me—

My childhood wasn't dying.

It was already dead.

And I had buried it without a fucking funeral.

10
The Identity Drift

I was only a couple months into seventh grade at Woodrow
when things really started to slip. My dad hadn't made it long
before he spiraled himself into prison, not jail. He was looking
at doing ten years.

It was supposed to be a big year for me in freedom. Science with
Mr. Moseman—legend had it we'd be dissecting a rat by spring.
Everyone else was buzzing about it, wide-eyed with curiosity or
queasy at the thought. The kind of milestone middle school
moment that had kids hyped up or ready to pass out.

Me? I was hobbling on one good ankle. Body, heart, and soul all
limping through the aftermath of a brutal year. I mean, losing
your dad to prison, your mom to death, and your ankle to
gravity? At some point, I started wondering if death was aiming
at me with a stormtrooper's aim.

When I got home from the hospital—because yeah, my ankle
was annihilated—I had one thing to look forward to: a teenage
church group trip I'd saved for myself. Just a weekend away, but
to me, it meant freedom. Friends. Des Moines. A food court and
the kind of reckless mall wandering that made you feel grown.
That weekend was the carrot I had been chasing for months.

But that broken ankle meant I wasn't going anywhere.

So, I did what any stubborn, aching kid does when the world
yanks the plan out from under him. I pivoted. I took the cash I
had saved and bought our first-ever DVD player. A couple
hundred bucks, easy. Nothing fancy. Not a Blu-ray, not a

surround-sound dream machine—just a straight up, state-of-the-art DVD player that felt like bringing the future home in a box.

The first movie I bought. Cast Away. Tom Hanks talking to a volleyball. Because of course I would.

And somewhere between Tom screaming "WILSON!" and me watching it alone in my room, I felt the drift begin. The slow, subtle current pulling me away from everything that used to feel steady.

I turned fourteen that school year. Spent most of it hobbling through hallways with crutches under my arms or my leg locked in one of those stiff black boots that made every step feel like a slap to the concrete. My body was healing, technically. But everything else? Still bruised. Still fragile.

That year, I reconnected with a kid I'd known from elementary school—Hector. We weren't close back then, just familiar faces on the same playground. But now? We talked. We laughed. We figured out how to navigate middle school chaos together. Hector had a girlfriend named Ashleigh—one of those sweet, early relationships where notes were folded like origami and handholding felt like marriage. They were learning how to be themselves. And so was I.

Then came the shift.

My mom made a decision that, on paper, was brave as hell. She went back to school. A bold move. A power move. Something that promised better days ahead for all of us.

But in the short term? It ripped the floor out from under me.

We moved out of the house—the one that had space, a backyard, history. The room my grandfather built with his bare hands. Gone. Swallowed by someone else's mortgage or memory. We traded it for a third-floor apartment that felt like a shoebox stacked in the sky.

Eight hundred square feet. Three bedrooms. One bathroom. Four growing kids, growing bills, and barely enough space to turn around without bumping into someone. We were crammed like a family photo someone folded in half.

And that wasn't the last move. By the time I turned fifteen, we moved again—this time to the west side. New zip code. New school. New everything. Every move meant another first day. Another lunchroom where I didn't know where to sit. Another hallway where I didn't know who to be. Every move, a new stage. Every stage, another version of myself I had to invent.

While it was all unfamiliar, I was lucky enough to find something solid tucked inside the chaos. Friendship.

Turned out, two other kids—Matt and Dimitri—were cousins with my cousin Ant. They were related through his dad's side. I was his cousin through his mom's. But that didn't matter. We didn't check bloodlines. We just claimed each other.

"Yeah, we're cousins," we'd say—like that was enough.

And it was. No questions. No barriers. We'd run around, laugh too loud, mess around like we'd grown up in the same living room. They let me in. Let me belong.

At a time when everything in my life felt unfamiliar and shaky, that small gesture meant everything.

And I wasn't just changing schools and addresses. I was shedding identities like old clothes, trying on different versions of myself like Halloween costumes. Hoping one day I'd find one that actually felt like home.

Here's the science behind the mess: my adolescent brain was still under construction. The prefrontal cortex—the part responsible for impulse control, emotional regulation, identity processing—was still a worksite full of tangled wires and warning signs. According to neuroscience, trauma during these formative years can hijack that process. It reprograms your wiring. Makes everything feel off-balance. Emotional levers get pulled at the wrong times. Trust misfires. Identity becomes a game of musical chairs with no music.

So yeah—hi, it's me. Dan. Your emotionally unstable, impulsive, risk-taking teenager.

I was fucking trying.

But I was unraveling, quietly. In the background. And my faith? Slipping through my fingers.

There I was—sitting in another church pew. Surrounded by believers praying in tongues, crying, reaching for a God I couldn't feel anymore. Then some guest preacher walks by, puts his hand on my shoulder, and says, "Don't turn your heart on God."

My mouth said, "Yes, sir."
But my eyes said, fuck you.

It wasn't rebellion. It was vacancy. I hadn't walked away from faith—it had slipped out the back door while I was trying to survive. There was no epic moment. No grand defiance. Just absence.

Faith didn't vanish overnight—it dissolved slowly, quietly. One unanswered prayer at a time.
One silence after another. It wasn't anger at God; it was exhaustion. It was realizing I was screaming into a void, tired of straining to hear whispers from a heaven that had stopped speaking back.

And in that silence, I drifted.

I floated from friend group to friend group like a lost tourist at the wrong bus station. Nerds. Church kids. The punk phase. The misfits. The troublemakers. I wore black for months, thinking if I looked dark enough on the outside, maybe it would match the storm inside. Every crowd came with a price—and most of the time, that price was me.

They laughed at me, and every chuckle landed like tiny blades against my heart, twisting, slicing. I felt my throat tighten, my face hot, shame searing its way across my skin. But I forced myself to laugh louder, hoping my own voice would drown out the humiliation burning in my chest.

I was the zombie friend. I was the walking pranked. Used me as the joke. I was the punchline they passed around like a shared secret. And I took it. Swallowed it. Laughed along because attention—even cruel attention—while I convinced myself it still felt better than being invisible.

Good group? Burned it.

71

Bad group? Let it burn me.

I let myself be roasted under a spotlight that never loved me back.

I became Chameleon from Spider-Man. Shifting. Adapting. Surviving in whatever world I landed in. But I wasn't choosing. I was reacting. I wasn't becoming who I wanted to be. I was becoming who I thought they needed.

Meanwhile, my dad was in prison.

We wrote letters, simple words scrawled in ink, smelling faintly of cigarettes or loneliness. But letters don't fill the empty chair at dinner, don't replace the steady hand on your shoulder when the world feels too heavy. I kept them folded tight, tucked away like secrets I wasn't ready to face. Letters don't listen. They don't notice when you start slipping. They don't tell you how to grieve. Or who to become.

My grandma had moved out of the city. My brothers were getting older. Everyone was stretched thin. Scattered.

And Diane?

Gone.

There was no adult pulling me aside. No mentor checking in. No one asking, "How are you holding up?" The ones who were supposed to guide me weren't just absent—they were shaping me into someone who would one day need to unlearn everything just to heal.

Instead of strengthening me as a child, they were weakening me as a man.

"It is easier to build strong children than to repair broken men."
—Frederick Douglass

That quote wasn't just wise. It was prophetic.

And I was already cracking.

11

Heroes on Separate Paths

He came back like he'd been carved out of concrete. My grandpa—fresh out of jail. And it wasn't just that he was back. It was who he was when he returned.

This man—this charming, smooth-talking, flirt-with-my-grandma-just-to-see-her-roll-her-eyes motherfucker—walked back into our lives like the gravity in the room owed him rent. And somehow, it felt like it did. His presence shifted the air. He spoke slower now, more intentional. Thought sharper.

He'd earned his GED while locked up, and you could tell he hadn't wasted the time. He was still funny as hell, still sharp with his one-liners, but something deeper had settled into him. A sense of purpose. A seriousness beneath the mischief. When he talked, people leaned in—not out of fear, but out of respect.

The family circled around him like planets around a sun. Even my grandma, who had every reason to shut him out, still let him pull a smile from her with just a look. He'd throw out something slick, and she'd roll her eyes like it annoyed her, but we all saw it—she still loved him. Still tethered to him in that way love sometimes refuses to let go.

And me?

I felt like I had a father again.

For the first time in years, there was a man in my life who showed up, who listened, who looked at me like I mattered.

There's a metaphor that fits here: stoning. Not biblical—emotional. When someone screws up, when they fall, when people decide they're done with you, they don't always come at you with fists. They come with silence. With shame. With judgment. It's death by disapproval. They bury you under the weight of everything you did wrong—and the worst part is, they make you hold the shovel.

But my grandpa didn't stay buried.

He picked up those stones and built something out of them. A second chance. A foundation. It wasn't perfect. But it was strong enough to stand on. And strong enough to help me stand, too.

I was feeling on top of the world again. And then, my mom pulled off a twist I never saw coming. For my sixteenth birthday, she surprised me with a limo. A whole-ass limousine. She coordinated it with some of my friends—Matt, Dimitri, and a few others. Torey wasn't running with our crew yet since he was still in middle school, but that night, rolling through town in that stretch limo like we ran the damn place? It was magic. It didn't matter that I had nothing figured out. That night, I felt seen. Celebrated. That ride through Sioux City felt like something out of a movie.

Rolling through Sioux City in that limo, I felt seen for the first time in forever—like someone had paused my chaos just long enough for me to feel worthy. It wasn't about the luxury—it was about the momentary certainty that I mattered, even briefly, in someone else's plans.

But I didn't realize then that the real gift was still coming. Because that same month, I met someone who would change everything. A friend who would shift the way I saw the world—and myself.

Travis.

He didn't walk into my life—he stormed in like we'd already been through a war together. Like we were picking up where something had paused, not starting something new. It wasn't a friendship. It was an instant brotherhood.

We met in study hall. Him half asleep, me half invisible. A few conversations later, he laid it out plain:

"Those dudes you hang with? The ones who clown on you and treat you like shit? I ain't about that. You wanna run with them, cool. But I'm out."

It wasn't dramatic. It wasn't said with heat. It was just real. And hearing someone stand up for me—without me asking, without it being a joke—meant everything. I dropped the other group. I ran with Travis from that moment forward.

The first night we hung out, we got high and headed back to where he was staying—his aunt's place. On the way back he looked up and said, "Beautiful moon tonight."

I laughed, "It's just the moon bro."

He smirked and shrugged one shoulder. "Maybe, still beautiful." That was Travis and that would be the first of hundreds of times I'd hear him say that.

When we got to his aunt's, we were stoned out of our minds, fumbling with the keys, trying to unlock the door. It wasn't working. Travis, in peak stoner logic, goes, "Bro, I'm just gonna lick the key."

"Homie," I told him, "that won't help."

But he kept licking the damn key anyway.

Then, of course, the door opened—and his aunt was standing right there.

"Who are you?" she asked, not mad, just... confused.

I froze. Full-on deer-in-headlights, heart-thudding-in-my-throat kind of freeze. Didn't say a word.

Travis, cool as hell, laughed and stepped in like it was no big deal. "This is Dan. He's cool." That was my first impression—two in the morning, high as shit, standing on someone's porch like an intruder trying to break in. And somehow, it still worked. That was the beginning of a what felt like a million inseparable weekends.

A few weeks later, I got into a fight at school. Well, "started" might fit better but I'm no wordsmith. I called a girl a bitch—yeah, I was in the wrong.

Mr. Jock Man, big dude, came up to me after and said, "She's like my little sister!"

I was already wound up, and his size didn't phase me. I said, "Oh."

Later I heard he had planned to find me with his jock friends after school, so I moved first. Spoiler alert: assumptions never help. I had assumed he'd make his move after school. So, I strategically make the first move and when he passes me in the hallway I stop and turned around.

I grabbed his shoulder, spun him around, and started swinging. Stupid move. But I was full of anger, and I didn't give a fuck what came next.

Another kid jumped in. Bigger. Stronger. I was getting my ass beat. Fists flying. The punches landed like lightning bolts, sharp, hot pain flashing across my face. Blood, metallic and warm, pooled in my mouth, but adrenaline muted everything. When Travis appeared—like a goddamn meteor crashing into the fight—my heart surged, the chaos muffled behind the roar of brotherhood finally showing up.

I was on the ground taking hits when I heard it:

"I got you, Dan!"

Travis came flying down the hallway. Kicked the behemoth off me. The guy turned and swung— hit Travis in the face like a fly running into a window.

Room froze. I smirked.

Travis didn't flinch. He fired back once and I swear to God he had the Iron Fist. Broke the dude's nose. Blood everywhere. Total chaos.

I got up, eyes wild, full on berserk mode, went after the original kid. Pinned him down and start again. Another giant, pushing six feet. I didn't care. Teachers yelling. Screaming. Total mayhem.

But in that moment, all I felt was this surge of
something I hadn't felt in years: Safety.

Because for once, I wasn't in the fight alone.

After that I did a day in juvenile detention and gave my mom
more stress than she was ready for. Turns out, the only thing
worse than getting your ass kicked in a hallway fight is trying to
explain to your mom why 'strategically starting' it was a good
idea.

But me and Trav, we were tight.

Pool halls after school. Ditching class. Late-night walks. Endless
runs to La Juanita's, where the burritos were so good they felt
like a religious experience. When Travis moved to Omaha, we
never stopped talking. Still called every day, still ran our mouths
like we were sitting across from each other.

Our families clowned us for how much we talked. Didn't matter.

That was my brother.

For once, I had someone who didn't want anything from me.
Who didn't try to fix me. Who just fucking showed up.

That first summer—the one we were supposed to tear up
together—he was gone. After Omaha, then to Tennessee to see
his dad. So I did something that surprised even me.

I joined summer school.

Not because I had to. I had the credits. Wasn't failing anything except maybe emotional regulation. But Ant and a few of the guys I rolled with were there, so I figured—why not?

That decision changed everything.

Even though I was the awkward white kid in the crew, they didn't treat me like an outsider. Ant was cousins with Matt, who was cousins with everybody, and when I rolled in, I wasn't Dan the misfit. I was Cousin Dan. And when you wore that title, it meant something. It meant if someone came at you, they were coming at all of us.

We weren't saints. Summer school was half babysitting, half rehab for kids on probation. Teachers with God complexes or teachers in trouble who got dumped there for a paycheck. But the environment didn't matter—we made it ours.

I told my grandpa I was thinking about joining. He just said, "Go talk to the people in charge." Diane would've said the same.

So I did. Walked up and told them I wanted extra credits. Threw in that my dad was in prison, and I was too young to get a real job, so it was this or the streets. They didn't know what to say. I didn't talk like a kid. I talked like someone who already had a lifetime under his belt.

They let me in.

That summer was all crunk music and arguments about hip-hop royalty. Lil Jon and the East Side Boyz. Tupac over Biggie. 50 Cent over Ja Rule. We all held firm that Eminem was one of the GOATs. The crew—Matt, Ant,

Dimitri, Torey—they became everything. Brothers. Survivors. Family forged in sweat and sarcasm.

For the first time in a long time, I felt my age.

We laughed. We fucked around. We learned just enough to keep it legit. One class taught me how to make a resume. I made one, walked into Taco Bell, and handed it in. They hired me on the spot. A few weeks later, I got Ashleigh, now more my friend than Hector was—hired too.

Bonus? I earned enough credits that I started thinking ahead. Like maybe I could graduate early. Maybe Travis and I could get an apartment. Escape. Baller shit.

While everyone else was stressing about homecoming, I was plotting my escape plan.

Because maybe, just maybe, if I moved fast enough—I could outrun the weight of everything chasing me.

Spoiler alert: I'd try that a lot.

It never fucking works.

After that summer, everything shifted. My cousins and I got scattered across different schools. We stayed close—still talked, still showed up—but I drifted back to Travis the second he came home.

There was no knocking at our houses. No asking. Just walking in. Our families understood—this wasn't friendship anymore. It was blood.

We'd hang at my grandpa's. Watch movies. Talk about life under the stars, passing a blunt between us like it was a baton in a relay we didn't want to end. He asked about Diane. About growing up in an evangelical house. The weight of it. The rules. The pressure. The shame.

And I asked about his dad. His siblings. His pain. The ghosts he carried.

I was the anime, comic, and video game nerd. He was the sports encyclopedia and history buff. Could call games like he'd already seen them. If ESPN had given him a mic back then, he would've owned it. He'd try to teach me.

"Bro, it's just percentages, patterns, adjustments."

"Nah," I'd say. "That's your world, not mine."

But I listened. Because that's what brothers do.

We were Winter Soldier and Captain America. Different paths. Same fight. Bound by something deeper than blood or background.

Time didn't matter. Distance didn't matter.

We had each other's back.

Always.

But that time didn't last forever.

Because soon, I'd be standing face-to-face with the one person I never expected to see again.

My dad.

Fresh out of prison.

Five hours away in Rapid City, South Dakota.

And somehow—I believed I could fix it. That I could bridge the gap. That maybe this time, I could be enough.

If Travis was Captain America—the steady, loyal, a man that inspired hope. That would make me the Winter Soldier.

Quiet. Feral. A survivor learning to feel again.

And I was ready for war.

Not with fists.

But for family.

12

A Death in Rapid City

I had a girlfriend named Michelle at the time, and even with Travis back in my life—showing up like the brother I'd always needed—it didn't quiet that fire in my gut to chase something that always felt just out of reach: my dad. I couldn't let go of the hope that maybe, just maybe, there was still something left to rebuild. A bond. A connection. A real father and son story that didn't end in silence and prison walls.

My grandpa had done the best he could to fill that role. Hell, he was doing everything he could with what he had. But those foundations I talked about? The ones that need to be reinforced after they're poured? My grandpa didn't have that. He came out of prison with a clean slate—but no structure to hold it. No scaffolding. No plan. And it collapsed quickly. He got evicted, and with him went everything he had—our memories in his belongings tossed to the curb like busted furniture.

Still, the hope wouldn't let go. I kept thinking: we'll talk about Diane. We'll keep her memory alive. We'll laugh about the same jokes, remember the same moments. Because no one else can do that the same way. Not Travis. Not Michelle. As much as they cared, as much as they showed up, they hadn't lived it. They didn't know Diane. Not the way I did. Not the way my dad did. And there's a weight to that kind of shared grief that only lives in shared blood.

When I told my mom I wanted to move to Rapid City and live with my dad, she looked at me with this flat, unreadable expression and said, "Are you sure? Because if you go out there, you're not coming back. You're not going to run from here to there and back again. If you want to go, then go."

No argument. No begging. Not even a, "If it doesn't work, we'll figure it out." Just... go.

I packed a duffel bag with everything I thought I'd need to start over. Spent what was left of my Taco Bell paycheck on a one-way Greyhound ticket. Put in my two weeks. The day came. Right on time. My mom gave me a hug as I said goodbye. I slung the bag over my shoulder, looked back one last time, and saw my mom give a little wave. Just a wave. Nothing more. Just a small flick of the hand, like she was waving off a stranger.

I climbed onto the bus, took a window seat, and jammed my duffel between the glass and my head. My Disc-man clicked to life, static fading into a burned mix of rap tracks that had become my heartbeat. I watched my city come to life—the skyline coming into focus as the bus departed—and told myself that what came next would be different.

As the bus pulled out of the parking lot, as the road began its stretch into the horizon and the sky deepens into gray, I caught one last glimpse of my mom, walking away from the station. Her shoulders slightly hunched, one hand brushing at her face. Was she crying? I told myself no. It was the wind. A hair in her eye. But I knew the truth. She wasn't saying goodbye because she'd already learned to let go.

"Objects in motion stay in motion unless acted upon by an outside force."

And I was in motion. Hurtling away from the grief I hadn't finished burying. Away from Diane.

85

Away from the weight of being the one left behind. I didn't know if this trip would fix anything. But I had to believe it might. I had to believe there was something in Rapid City that would make sense of it all.

When I finally arrived, it was later in the day than I expected. My dad picked me up and took me straight to the high school to finish my enrollment. No welcome to your new home. No excitement of this new journey. Just a side-hug, a "Glad you're here," and the steady silence of a man too detached to care—or maybe too wounded to show it.

The next morning, I was up before my alarm. The house was cold and dark. Mountain Time hung heavy in my bones. I shuffled into the kitchen, poured black coffee into a chipped mug, and flipped on the TV.

"The unidentified remains of a man were found this morning in what appears to be a homicide…" the anchor said, casual as a weather report.

I stared at the screen and thought: Death is always walking next to me.

Days blurred. Between school and work, my life became a series of muted routines. If my dad was home, we ate in silence—steak or chicken, a starch, a vegetable. Same dinner. Same stiffness. The house was spotless. Not Diane-clean. This was different. Clinical. Cold. Like he had traded connection for control.

There was no landline. Only his cell phone. One phone. One link to the life I had left behind. If I wanted to call Sioux City, I had to ask. I rarely did.

The man I was living with—the man who was supposed to be my father—felt like a stranger with the same DNA pulsing in his veins. And even though I had learned how to carry myself, how to speak like an adult, how to read a room and mirror emotion, none of it worked here. This wasn't a room. It was a minefield.

Tension mounted like a storm waiting for a trigger.

One night, I mentioned Diane. Just a passing memory. Something gentle. Something real.

He waved it off like I'd just said something inconvenient. Like I'd asked to change the channel during a game.

The tears came fast. Sharp. Uninvited.

"What's your problem?" he asked, like I was the one being unreasonable.

"My problem?" I said, voice cracking. "I left everything behind to sit in a seven-by-nine-foot box with someone who doesn't even look at me. I should've stayed in Iowa. This was a fucking joke."

He called me ungrateful. Told me I wasn't going back.

That was that.

I buried it. Buried myself. Went to school. Went to work. Came home. Said nothing. On nights he was gone—usually with his girlfriend—I'd eat in silence, stare out the window, listen to music, and wonder if this was what prison felt like.

He always seemed broke. No car payment. No child support. Still broke. Sometimes he asked me for money. If I gave it, he'd buy me cigarettes like that made us even.

After that first fight, we tried to reset. Went to a movie. Small talk. Then he told me I needed to learn to budget. That if I wanted snacks or clothes, I'd need to pay for them myself. I didn't mind. I understood independence. I'd been buying my own shit for years.

But then I ate one of his Little Debbie oatmeal pies.

And he lost it. Screamed like I'd cracked open his bank account. Raged like I'd betrayed some sacred trust.

"You're acting more like an annoyed older brother than a dad," I said, voice low, tired.

The silence that followed hit harder than any insult. It said everything.

By spring, I was counting the days until my trip back to Iowa. But then a C on my report card threatened to cancel it. I paid a kid twenty bucks to change it to a B.

I handed it to my dad like it was real.

He glanced. Grunted. Let it slide.

But I should've known.
Two days before my trip, he stormed into my work. Taco Bell. Full rage.

"Get in your fucking car. Now."

Then to my manager: "He's done."

Just like that—I was fired. In front of everyone. Humiliated. Stunned. I sat in the car, heart pounding.

"What the fuck just happened?"

"You're a lying piece of shit," he spat. "Your mom got the real report card."

We got home. I stepped out of the car, still in uniform. He stormed over, yanked the hood open, and ripped the spark plugs out of my engine.

"In case you try to be slick," he said, smirking like he'd just won something.

I felt my body move before I thought.

"Fuck you, Bob."

He turned and swung. Fist to face.

His fist hit my jaw with the sickening crack of bone meeting bone, lights exploding behind my eyes. For a split second, the world blurred into red and black pulses. My mouth filled with a metallic tasting syrup; my breath came ragged—but the physical pain was nothing compared to the sudden, raw clarity: this wasn't a fight. This was goodbye.

Maybe that's what hit me. Maybe it was what came after. But something in me broke wide open.

I lunged. Missed. Clipped his leg. We both went down hard. In the scramble, my pants tore wide open.

I stood there—chest heaving, face burning, clothes ripped—staring at a man I didn't recognize anymore.

"I hate you," I said.

He looked at me, shrugged. "Welp. Get in line, bud."

That was it.

He turned me in to the school. In-school suspension. A week in a cubicle. No contact. No conversation. No life.

I called Michelle. Hoping for comfort. Hoping for someone to tell me I wasn't crazy.

She didn't yell. She didn't even pause.

"Why would you do that?" she asked. "You messed this up. Not your dad."

And she was right.

Her words sank deep—straight through my anger, pride, denial. The gentle clarity in her voice didn't burn; it sliced quietly, precisely, like a scalpel removing infection. I swallowed hard, realizing this wasn't blame—it was belief. She saw more in me than I did, and it hurt because it meant I had to face myself.

That was the first time I really understood accountability. Not the kind that comes from punishment—but from love. From someone you trust saying, "You're better than this. Own your shit."

A few weeks later, I got my job back. Same uniform. Same crew. Same grease-stained jokes. But something had shifted. I was back—but I wasn't the same.

There was no tearful apology from my dad. No healing moment. No redemption arc. Just silence. The kind that thickens like fog and never lifts.

Then he announced I'd be quitting Taco Bell. Said I'd be working construction with him that summer. I said no. He said it wasn't a question.

But I'd already made my move before he ever said the words. A bus ticket sat folded in my wallet—my so-called "vacation." Four days in Sioux City. That's all I needed. Just enough time to lay low, regroup, and start crafting a new plan. A new talk track. A way to stay for good.

Somewhere between towns, as the wheels of the Greyhound hummed against the pavement and the world passed in gray and green blurs, I leaned against the window and stared at my own reflection. I didn't know what I was expecting when I left for Rapid City—but it sure as hell wasn't to feel like a burden. As the bus hummed beneath me, every mile felt heavier, my reflection distorted in the dark glass. Why did I ever think this would heal us? Diane was gone. Our bond had unraveled long before this Greyhound hit the highway. All that remained were tangled threads, too knotted to fix.

I thought there was supposed to be something unbreakable between a father and a son. Something sacred. Something solid.

But this? This wasn't sacred. It wasn't even stable. It was toxic. Tension, silence, walking on eggshells just to make it through the day. And where the hell was all the money he worked so hard for? It disappeared into excuses and smoke.

And now here I was, heading back. And I knew what people would say. That I was running. Again.

But they never talked about the first run—the one I made toward him. Toward redemption. Toward hope. I wasn't running from something. I was running to it. Hoping to fix it. Hoping to find something worth saving.

Now, this second run? This one was different. This one was about survival. Because when you're drowning, you don't wait for someone to learn how to swim—you get the fuck out of the water.

People say I was running like it was cowardly. But maybe they just stayed in shitty situations longer than they should've. Maybe they called it loyalty because calling it fear would hurt too much.

When I got there, I'd talk to Mom. I'd follow the rules. She gave me the list, and I accepted it without flinching: Church three times a week. A job. If I had a girlfriend, she was only allowed at the house. Fair. Structured. Survivable.

I walked into Taco Bell like I never left. Found Rachel, my old manager. Asked if I could have my job back.

She didn't blink. "When?"

"Three days."

She smiled. "See you then, bud."

That was it. My mom granted me with her approval. But before it was official, she said one more thing:

"You get to tell your dad." I didn't even hesitate. I picked up the phone, called him, and told him I was leaving.

He exploded. Raged.

I let him vent while I didn't listen. We hung up without saying goodbye.

I went to Travis's. I went where love didn't have a leash.

The morning, I left Rapid City, I crammed my entire life into the back of my car—duffel bags packed like puzzle pieces, my entire bedroom folded into the backseat. I barely slept the night before, too wired with anticipation to close my eyes for more than a few minutes. I had it all timed down to the minute: leave at 8:00 a.m., pull into Sioux City by 2:00 p.m., link up with Trav, and clock in for my shift at Taco Bell by 10:00 p.m. sharp.

He passed me at the door as I was walking out. "Love you," I said.
He didn't even look up. "Yep."

I left anyway. Windows down, music up, heart cracked open just wide enough to let a little hope in. For a moment, it felt like forward motion. Like maybe this time would be different.

But thirty minutes down the road, the engine coughed, sputtered, and died all while the dashboard was lighting up like a goddamn

Christmas tree. I coasted to the shoulder, climbed out, and walked until I found a payphone. I called the only number I had.

He showed up, parked, sighed as he walked pass me, and went right for my car. At this point, calling it a car felt generous. It was less vehicle, more emotional metaphor on wheels—broken, patched together, barely functional, yet somehow still dragging itself down the road.

Didn't say much. Just popped the hood, looked it over, and muttered, "Alternator."

We hit the parts store. Then we headed to the library for diagrams. Then back to the highway the entire time in awkward silence. With semis screaming past us he leaned over the engine, fixing what he could on the side of the interstate. Once it was fixed I thought, "Ok, no more problems. Almost home."

 Two hours later, another setback—a flat tire. I tried to change it myself. I knew how. I had a spare. But the lug nuts were shot. No tools, no extras. The two I tried taking off snapped under pressure. That's when I made the second call—one I didn't want to make.

He showed up again, jaw tight, quiet. The kind of silence that says I told you so without saying a word. Then he bent down, braced himself, and tried to finish the job. And just like I said—snap.
Snap. Another one. His silence turned from frustration into something else. Not anger. Maybe resignation.

Two more hours. Five new lug nuts. One working tire.

I had $170 to my name. I gave him a hundred. Kept seventy. I knew how to stretch it. By the time I rolled into Sioux City, the day was nearly gone. But I pulled into the Taco Bell parking lot, still clocked in five minutes early, and walked through those doors like nothing had happened.

And just like that—I was home.

And standing behind that greasy Taco Bell counter, I realized I'd been mourning something already dead. I'd gone to Rapid City hoping for rebirth—but instead, found only the grave. That father-son bond wasn't fragile; it wasn't strained. It was dead. Cold. Final. Buried under a lifetime of silence in Rapid City.

13
Defying the Odds

I was fucking back, baby.

Travis was Cap—steady, resilient, determined. And me? I was still Bucky Barnes, fighting my past, forging a future, waiting for the next fight even when peace was right in front of me. Together, we were more than comic heroes, we were momentum in human form—speeding forward, defying gravity, inertia, and every law of fate written to slow us down.

Windows down. Music blasting. Trav riding shotgun. We weren't just cruising—we were storming into our own version of freedom. The world didn't expect us to make it. Every number, every statistic, every headline said we were supposed to be a cautionary tale.

Did you know that in the U.S., over 17.6 million children— nearly one in four—grow up without a father in the home? And of those kids?

• 85% are more likely to struggle with behavioral disorders.
• 71% more likely to drop out of high school.
• 63% more likely to attempt suicide.

Those stats? They had our names written all over them. But we didn't give a damn. Travis and I made an unspoken pact: we were going to break every, last one of them. Line by line. Statistic by statistic. We weren't becoming the story—they were.

That summer, it was all we talked about—those numbers. Travis had this mind wired for stats. Sports. Sociology. School. He soaked in data like most people soaked in sunlight. Once he got me hooked, we were off. We debated everything. Quarterbacks. Batting averages. Rapper rankings. The fucking weather. He liked T.I., so I backed Lil' Flip out of spite. Half the time we didn't even believe our side—we just wanted to argue. It sharpened us. Strengthened us. Made us better. Made us brothers.

But that summer held more than just friendly fire. It held something quieter, heavier.

My grandma was living in Beresford, South Dakota, preparing to pack up and move to Tennessee. Before she left, I met her for lunch at a little roadside diner just off I-90. The kind of place where the booths were worn soft from decades of stories and the coffee tasted like regret but came with free refills. We sat across from each other, the low hum of old country music filling the spaces between our words, the air heavy with grease and the scent of sun-warmed vinyl.

We laughed. Talked about Rapid. School. What was next. It was light. Familiar.

Then she looked up from her plate, eyes steady and full of something that was heavy but had to be said.

"I still can't believe your dad would treat his own son that way."

Her voice was soft, but her words hit like a hammer. Not because I didn't already know. But because someone else said it out loud. Someone who saw me. Believed me. She called it what it was. No sugar. No filters. Just truth—wrapped in love. And in that moment, I felt it deep in my chest: permission to hurt. To not have to keep pretending.

And I wasn't alone.

My grandpa had started showing up more too. He'd found himself a modest place he could afford, and for the first time in a long time, he felt steady. He was present. Available. Real. There was a rhythm in my life again. A pulse. And I wasn't about to give that up.

That same year, my younger brother Josh met a kid who'd become his best friend—their friendship mirrored mine and Travis's in a way that felt too perfect to be coincidence. Two brothers, each finding a brother in someone else. Back then, it just felt cool. Later, it would feel like fate planting seeds we didn't yet know we'd need.

But right then? I had my license. A beat-up car. And freedom. At least until the car finally gave out. That's when Grandpa stepped in. He passed me the keys to … his white Chrysler—a '95 or '96, a bruised-up beast with a crooked cassette deck—but to me, it was a spaceship, like the one Diane promised when I was 12. I swear to God my life is a constant series of cycles and patterns.

He couldn't keep up the payments anymore, so I took it over for the cost of the loan. I added subwoofers, cranked up Slim Thug and Chamillionaire, and turned that old Chrysler into a sound system on wheels. Travis and I lived in it—cruising late at night, debating physics and music, dreaming about everything that might come next.

Sliding into that old Chrysler felt like stepping onto a launchpad. Every rumble of the engine, every bass-heavy beat pulsing from the subwoofers, every mile we drove—it wasn't just distance. It was defiance. It was victory. Every late-night cruise felt like we were rewriting the maps that said we wouldn't make it.

Somewhere in that haze of independence and breakneck speed, Michelle and I broke up. Not with grace. Not with maturity. I just stopped talking to her. She asked if we were done, and I said yeah.

Looking back now, that silence wasn't strength—it was cowardice disguised as detachment. I wish I'd done better by Michelle. I wish I'd had the courage to face endings as fiercely as beginnings.

I think back and cringe at the kid I was. Years later, I think I apologized. I hope I did. I meant to.

The rest of that year blurred into laughter and late nights. Basketball courts. Pool halls. Cheap snacks at 2 a.m. Travis's aunt had a pool, and we were always there—floating, roasting each other, chasing girls, eating chips with sunburned shoulders and chlorine-stung eyes. Eventually, I got Travis a job with me at Taco Bell. Ashleigh was already there, so the three of us became a pack. We worked together, closed together, rode home together. Graveyard shifts. Post-shift feasts. 4 a.m. drop-offs when Travis called me freezing on the curb, waiting for someone to remember he existed.

We were the kids with nowhere to be, but everywhere to go.

Then—like life does—it shifted.

My mom said we were moving again. Ponca, Nebraska. Just far enough to be exile. I was supposed to switch schools, quit work, start over. Again. But I had just built something worth holding. I made the only move I could.

I moved out.

I talked to my Aunt Kim and Uncle Jim. Asked if I could rent their basement spare room. I paid my own way. Kept my job. Stayed in Sioux City. Saw Travis whenever I wanted. No curfews.
No cages. No one telling me who I could be or where I could go. I'd made it out of Rapid City. Out of that silence. Out of that chaos. And I wasn't going back.

That's when Ashley #2 entered the picture. We started talking, and somewhere in the conversation, we realized our families had known each other for years. We'd even played together as toddlers in my grandpa's front yard. Neither of us remembered it, but she remembered him. That was enough for me.

Meanwhile, my bond with Grandpa deepened. We'd talk about everything—money, family, cars, and mysteries of the universe. One afternoon, he made me promise him three things:

1. **Protect those closest to you—especially women.**
2. **Be someone people can count on. Be honest. Be resourceful.**
3. **See the world. Get out of Iowa. Live.**

Then he asked for one more promise. One I couldn't give.

"Promise me you won't join the military," he said, his voice softer than I'd ever heard it. "I can't lose anyone else. Not after Jeff. Not you too, Danny."

I nodded. I said I'd try. But I couldn't promise him that. Not after 9/11. Not after everything. I'd already made my own vow, silently, years ago. I carried it like a secret mission—quiet, steady, burning.

Still, I carried his words like a stone in my pocket.

Later, when I told him what happened in Rapid City—about my dad—he was livid. This man, pushing sixty, struggling to breathe with a smoker's cough and oxygen tanks nearby, was ready to drive across state lines to throw hands.

That was my grandpa. Unfiltered. Unapologetic. Fierce in the ways that mattered most.

One day, he walked into Taco Bell to collect a car payment. He wore a tank top tight across his chest, tufts of chest hair peeking out, purple wind pants swishing, and those black cowboy boots clicking like declarations across the tile. I saw him and lit up. Travis burst out laughing.

"Love the boots, Greg!"

My grandpa, cool as ever, chuckled through his cigarette-husky voice. "They're the most comfortable things I own. Don't give a damn how they look."

I slipped him some food, and we chatted for a bit. That was him. Just showing up. Just being exactly who he was.

But there was more than humor in him. There was pride. One night, Travis and I came home after a shift. Still buzzing from our latest debate—black holes vs wormholes, the possibility of time travel, whether humans would ever escape Earth—we stumbled into the kitchen where Grandpa was already sitting, cigarette burning, smoke curling like stories above his head.

We grabbed chairs. Lit our own. Sat with him like it was sacred. We talked about school. Grades. Girls. Physics. Life. He didn't say much. Just listened. Let the conversation pour like coffee into silence.

Then, before he left, he looked at me and said it plain.

"I'm proud of you, Danny. You're doing good. Real good. And don't worry about the rest of those car payments. A grandson staying in school, staying out of trouble, doing what you're doing—he shouldn't have to worry about petty shit like that."

He stood. Hugged me. Walked out the door.

No drama. No big gesture.

Just love.

And it stuck with me.

Not just because of what he said—but how he said it. Like I was more than surviving. Like I was finally living.

That was the year I exhaled. After all the grief. All the fights. All the broken homes and promises—that was the year I felt whole again.

But life has a way of slowing you down. Of reminding you how fragile it all really is.

That reminder came in October, when Chris died.

Chris wasn't just some name in the yearbook. He was family to Travis. Not by blood—but by presence. By history. He was Brian's friend. Brian was Travis's older cousin. Wherever Brian went, Chris wasn't far behind. A fixture. A big brother. A legend in their orbit.

I didn't know him well. We'd shared a few nods. A couple of "What's ups." But Travis? Travis looked up to him. Ashleigh did, too. They carried that loss like a cracked rib—quiet, invisible, but every breath hurt.

At the funeral, grief hung thick in the air, heavy as summer humidity. I stared through tear filled eyes at Travis's shoulders rise and fall sharply, his breath catching with every inhale, eyes fixed on a point nobody else could see. My chest tightened, a lump forming in my throat for the grief my brother felt. The quiet sobs around me became a quiet symphony of pain. Even the air tasted bitter, tinged with loss.

Watching Travis grieve felt like staring into a black hole, powerless, seeing something immense and inevitable consume him piece by piece, knowing there was nothing I could do to pull him back out.

Then I slowly remembered what Diane taught me. You don't need to fix the pain. You just need to sit with it. Be there. Let the silence speak. So I did.

Seventeen years old, already too familiar with graves and grief, I thought I'd know what to do. So I tried.

I asked questions. I listened. I tried.

But watching Travis grieve cracked something in me I didn't know still had seams.

I was willing and ready to trade places with him. I would've taken it for him. I would've done anything to fix what couldn't be fixed.

And I didn't know—couldn't have known—that this loss was just the rehearsal. That the next one would hollow out everything we had left.

I didn't know that this would be the last summer I'd ever have him.

14
The Day the World Went Quiet

There are a few chapters in this book that are hard to even start… and this is definitely one of them.

Because life had been good. Like—really good.

While Travis and Ashleigh were learning how to live with what had happened to Chris, our circle pulled in closer. Tighter. Like we all knew, even if we didn't say it out loud, that we had to hold on to each other while we still could. We moved together like a unit—wounded but intact. Still reeling. Still rising.

Travis and I were wrapping up our junior year. Ashleigh was finishing her senior year. We were counting down the months until summer like it was going to save us. And maybe it did. At least for a little while.

I focused on Travis. I kept him talking about Chris—his stories, his memories, the little things that made him real. I didn't have answers. I didn't try to fix anything. I remembered what Diane taught me: you don't need to solve pain. You just have to make space for it. So that's what I did… not knowing he'd be doing the same for me soon.

And when I didn't know what else to say, I'd look at him and say, "One day at a time, man."

I don't even know where I got it from—some book, a movie, maybe just something I overheard once—but it stuck. And Travis, in only the way he could, would nod and say, "Yeah well… sometimes it's just one foot in front of the other."

That was it. That was our rhythm.

Him and me. Processing the past while sprinting into the present. Reconstructing ourselves one inside joke, one meal, one long conversation at a time.

I was back.

Junior year. Living free. Working. Driving. Eating burgers with my best friend, talking shit and debating life like we were philosophers in some 17-year-old punk rock version of a think tank. For the first time in years, I wasn't surviving, I was living.

That year, I was locker partners with Ashleigh. Travis had decided to go to Central—a smaller high school across town. Of course he did. That's the thing about Travis—if you went left, he went right. If you got an iPhone, he'd get an Android out of spite. If we were at North, he was going to Central, where the graduating class was small enough to feel like family.

And me and Ashley? We were his unofficial Uber before Uber existed. He didn't have a car, so we were always swooping him up. We'd grab him after school and hit La Juanita's, Jim's Burgers, or Johnny Mars. I can still see him at Johnny's, ordering chicken strips without shame and asking the waitress for a salad bowl full of barbecue sauce. Not a ramekin. A whole damn bowl. "Charge me extra—I don't care," he'd say. And he meant it.

That was our vibe. Carefree. Messy. Beautiful.

And then it all blew up.

We'd just gone to breakfast—Horizon, our usual spot. Travis had a shift at Taco Bell later, so I dropped him off, gave him a nod, told him I'd catch him later. Just another normal day. When I walked into my place, I saw my Aunt Kim sitting at the kitchen table. The landline was in her hand. Her mouth was covered. Her eyes wide, swollen with tears. The cord hung from the wall like it had just dropped from Heaven.

I froze.

Something in me just knew.

She looked up and whispered, "Danny... Dad is dead."

The moment she said he was gone, the world collapsed into silence—like all the air had suddenly vanished, leaving behind a vacuum where no sound could travel, no breath could fill my lungs.

I blinked, trying to understand. "What do you mean?" I found the air to ask, stupidly, because that's what your brain does when it doesn't want to believe what your body already knows.

"Danny," she said again, louder this time. "Dad is gone."

Then she turned away, sobbing, trying to call the next person on her list. Like grief had a roster she needed to get through before she could fall apart completely.

The air felt suddenly thick, impossible to breathe. My ears rang, a high-pitched whine drowning out every other sound. I staggered onto the front porch, gripping the railing, knuckles white, heart hammering like it wanted to escape my chest— because maybe then the pain would leave too.

It felt like I was reliving a horror story from four years ago—only this time, it wasn't Diane.

This time it was him.

My grandfather.

One of my anchors. My north star.

The first person I called was my girlfriend, Ashley. I told her my grandpa had died.

Her voice didn't crack. There was no pause. Just a flat, "Oh wow. Really?" Like I had just told her something mildly interesting. Like I'd said I got a new shirt. She said she'd come by after work. I called Travis next.

And he cried.

Not because he had a deep relationship with my grandpa. He didn't. He cried because I cried. Because he knew what that man meant to me. Travis didn't just hear the words—I felt them land in his chest. He let the grief in with me.

And that… that is the difference.

My grandpa had just hugged me five days earlier. Told me he was proud of me. June 23rd. The last time I saw him alive.

Now, I was on my way to the hospital with my Aunt Kim—driving in the very car my grandpa had helped me get. The car that had carried Travis and me across town a hundred times. And as if it knew the chapter had ended, it died right there in the hospital parking lot. Just shut down. Never started again. I never drove it again.

When the car died in that parking lot, I almost laughed bitterly through a tear- and snot- covered face. Of course, it gave out here. Like it knew its purpose had ended, its journey tied inseparably to the man who'd given it life. The car wasn't just metal and rubber—it was memories, freedom, and now, a gravestone.

Inside, the family was wrecked. My mom. My uncles. My aunt. Everyone sobbing. Faces twisted by disbelief and pain. I don't remember who else was there. Everything was muffled. Like I was underwater, barely holding my breath. My grandpa was only sixty. Just sixty. My great grandparents had lived into their eighties, and even though watching them die was hard, their deaths came with some sense of completion. A full life. A closing chapter.

But this? This felt like someone had ripped out the final pages and lit them on fire.

Because this wasn't just my grandfather. This was the man who stepped in when my father stepped out. The man who carried me when no one else could. Who built me a room. Who gave me a name.

And now he was gone.

Funerals have a funny way of attracting people who never bothered to visit when it mattered. Like they thought grief was some weird social event where attendance could earn them extra points in the afterlife.

At the funeral, the air inside the service home felt different. Thick. Tense. Like the walls themselves were grieving. People stood around in hushed tones—some genuine, some pretending. There were hugs, awkward silence, forced memories. A few people sobbing harder than they ever showed love while he was still here.

I watched them—the people crying louder and I judged them because in his worse times most of these people weren't around. And beneath my grief rose anger, quiet and hot. Why couldn't they see him when he was here? Why did death always have to clear their vision?

We walked in as a family, took our seats in the front row. The row where the weight lived. Where memories clung to every breath.

I remember trying to stay present, but my mind drifted. Then I saw him.

My aunt Kim's ex-husband had shown up. The man had worked side by side with my grandpa for years—sweating through drywall jobs, building things together. He walked up, gave her a hug, said "I'm sorry," and sat down. No drama. No performance. Just shared history showing up for shared pain.

And right behind him? Uncle Jim—her current husband—looking like someone had slapped the jealousy across his face. His whole body shifted, like that one hug had knocked him off center.

It was petty. It was human. And it was fucking ridiculous.

We were burying her father. The man who helped raise me. And you're mad because the ex who actually knew him showed respect?

Later, I told Travis. He shook his head.

"Grief," he said, "makes people show their truest selves."

And he wasn't wrong.

Some carry you.
Some make it about them.
Some show up too late.

But you never forget who was who. When the service ended, we stood as a family, row by row, filing out like tradition said we should. I remember rising, my legs heavy like sandbags. The chapel had gone silent, just the creak of pews and rustling fabric as we moved.

To my right, Ashley sat with her dad, her face blank, unreadable. She looked like she was watching a movie she didn't quite understand.

But to my left?

There was Travis.

And he wasn't composed. He wasn't trying to hold it together. His face was swollen. Eyes red. Ashleigh—his support, our friend—was standing next to him, holding his arm like she was anchoring him to the earth.

Seeing Travis's tears broke something deeper inside me. Not because it hurt—but because reassured me that I wasn't alone. He wasn't just watching my pain; he was carrying it with me, refusing to let me drown beneath its weight.

And in that moment, I didn't just see him—I felt him.

He wasn't grieving my grandpa. He was grieving me.

He was feeling my loss like it was his own.

Our eyes met. One breath, maybe two. But it said everything:

"I'm here. You don't have to fall alone."

I turned away. Not because I didn't want to see it. But because if I didn't, I was going to break into a million fucking pieces in front of everyone.

Grief reveals people.

Not just who they are in pain, but who they are when you're in pain.

At the burial, the Navy showed up and gave him full honors. A twenty-one-gun salute. Folded flag. The works. A gesture of respect for a life that didn't get enough of it when he was alive.

People I hadn't seen in years showed up—crying, hugging, making speeches they'd never have made if he was still breathing. They had stories. They had tears. But they didn't have time for him when it would've mattered most.

I wanted to scream.

But I didn't.

I just sat there. And I grieved.

I carried the casket. I was a pallbearer. I lowered him into the ground with dirt on my shoes and silence in my soul.

And no one—no one—understood what I lost like Travis did.

That summer, we were inseparable. If I wasn't with my family, I was with him. We sat by his pool. Talked late. Walked by the river at 1 a.m. Ate breakfast at Horizon before the sun even thought about rising.

He didn't try to fix me.

He just stayed.

That's what grief needs. Not answers. Not solutions. Just presence. Someone willing to sit in the silence. In the ache. In the fucking hole it leaves behind.

And science backs it up.

Studies have shown that the presence of close friendships during grief drastically reduces the risk of prolonged grief disorder. Not because friends erase the pain—but because they carry some of it. They let it move. They help you breathe.

Travis gave my grief a place to go.

He helped me stay afloat. Even when I couldn't feel my own heartbeat.

He didn't need to understand every detail.
He just needed to be there.

And he was.

I started that summer wrecked. Angry. Abandoned.

But I wasn't alone.

Because grief, when shared, doesn't weigh as much.

And love—real love, brother love, the kind that stays even when it doesn't know what to say— doesn't ask you to heal.

It just holds the pieces.

That summer began with grief carving me hollow, but Travis filled those empty spaces with his presence. He didn't offer solutions or empty words—he offered himself, standing next to me in the wreckage, holding the broken pieces until I could carry them again.

15
The Last Summer

It's wild when you look back and realize all the things you didn't know you were doing for the last time. The last Friday night you crashed on a friend's living room floor. The last time you picked up a GameCube controller or passed around a PlayStation after school. The last time you logged into a video game lobby and waited for your best friend's username to pop up. The last time you texted someone you thought would be in your life forever. The last time a phone call ended like it was just another day— never knowing it was goodbye.

If I had known those were goodbyes, maybe I would've said more. Or maybe I wouldn't have said anything at all. Maybe I would've just held on a little longer. Maybe I would've memorized the way it all felt.

Some losses you can see coming. When my great-grandparents passed, there was time. The grieving came in slow waves, like leaves letting go in autumn. The goodbye felt natural. Expected. Like it had earned its place.

But there are other times when life doesn't ask for permission. It just flips the fucking table midmeal and leaves you staring at the wreckage.

What I didn't know—what I couldn't have known—was that the summer after my grandfather died would be the last summer I'd have Travis. And sometimes, that's all there is.

That summer, we didn't leave each other's side. We were both grieving—him for Chris, me for my grandfather—and in the middle of all that pain, we became each other's anchor. My grief was fresh, raw, still throbbing in places I didn't know could hurt, and Travis carried it with me. He made space for my sadness. Let me talk. Let me vent. Let me crumble. He didn't make it about him, even though he was still reeling, too. He didn't try to fix it—he just stood in it with me. He was glue when I felt like dust.

And I tried to be the same for him.

But grief doesn't pause the world. While I was drowning in the weight of what I'd lost, Travis still had a life too. A father in Tennessee. A different story. One that wasn't mine to tell. And when the time came, he left to spend time with him.

Before he left, he looked at me and said, "Why don't you just come with me?"

We talked about it. Really talked. Not just about seeing his dad. My grandma had just moved from South Dakota to Tennessee, too. The idea started to take shape—a month-long road trip. Two kids, one car, chasing down something like peace.

It felt real. Like something we could actually do.

And I should've fucking done it.

But I didn't.

I didn't know why for a long time I stayed back. Maybe I told myself it wasn't the right time. Maybe I thought his dad wouldn't want me there. Maybe I was just afraid to leave the grief behind, even for a little while. Either way—I stayed.

Looking back now, I realize every excuse I gave myself was rooted in fear—fear of losing my grip on grief, fear of chasing peace only to never find it. I'd later realize the worst regret wasn't what I did—it was everything I didn't do when I had the chance.

I told Travis I was fine. Lied straight through my teeth. I wasn't fine. I was floating through days like a ghost. Half-there. Half-aware. I needed something to hold onto. Someone.

Ashley—my girlfriend at the time—became that someone. We had just started working together at this fast-food place, and during those two weeks Travis was gone, I pretty much moved into her house. Her parents had rules—I stayed in a separate room, went camping with them, kept the "good kid" act running—but I was there constantly. I needed the stability.

And I talked to her dad, Dave. A lot.

Dave had known my grandfather. Worked with him back in the day. We'd trade stories. His raspy voice would echo memories of a man with cocky swagger and a crooked grin who rolled dice on life like he always had the odds stacked in his favor. That man had charisma before TikTok turned it into a commodity.

In a way, Dave stepped into the gap. A man who knew the version of my grandpa I never got to meet. Stoic. Strong. Solid. And Pam—Ashley's mom—she was the soft landing I didn't know I needed. She cried in front of me. Felt things out loud. Loved without conditions.

After Diane. After Grandpa. After everything—it felt like home.

But safety, when you haven't had it, can become a drug. It clouds everything. It convinces you that proximity is love. That warmth is connection. Years later, I'd realize that I wasn't in love with Ashley—I was in love with her family. With the idea of being part of something solid again. I had been chasing that feeling since the '90s, since before the funerals and fights and fractured homes.

And that chase would come with a cost.

Going into my senior year I had all those summer school credits stacked up. I could've graduated early. Instead, I worked the system to finish by noon every day. It gave me time—to breathe, to work, to be with Ashley… and Travis, who rigged his schedule the same way.

We both would get out of school by noon and lived like kings of the afternoon.

The fall of our senior year, we were hit with the Iowa Standardized Tests—the annual torture session. No one cared except the teachers. They'd bribe us with snacks like that was going to unlock our full potential.

Travis had to take the test at Central. And here's the part that still makes me laugh…

He scored NUMBER ONE in the entire state.

And he didn't even try. The mayor showed up to shake his hand. The local paper called him a genius. Travis? He basked in it like a cat in the sun. "You know I piss excellence, right?" he'd say, full smirk. "You're looking at the smartest guy you know."

And he wasn't wrong.

He was effortlessly brilliant.

The rest of the year was a balancing act. Relationship. Best friend. Job. Bills. Car. I moved out of Kim and Jim's place and into my own apartment—the same building where my grandfather had passed away. It felt right, like claiming something. Like keeping him close.

Sometimes Travis would crash at my place. I'd make sure we got to school on time—or not. His aunt would call and chew me out for letting him sleep in. We'd laugh about it, shrug, do it again. We made it through. We graduated.

I started working at a cell phone kiosk in the mall. Travis was still working at Taco Bell. We had picked up construction gigs with Ashley's dad—ripping out walls, swinging hammers, tearing down the past to make space for something new. Nothing made more sense to us than destruction that had a purpose.

And then, it happened.

A recruiter from the Army National Guard walked by my kiosk and stopped mid-stride.

"Aren't you Borchers?"

I blinked. "Yeah… how do you know that?"

"I met you freshman year. Rock climbing challenge. You told me to come find you senior year."

I had forgotten. He hadn't.

That moment lit a fuse in me. I remembered the promise I made—to myself, to my grandfather. I couldn't give him all four promises; I'd have to break at least one. This was the first and only recruiter to talk to me. It didn't matter if he was Marine, Navy, or Army. It didn't matter if it was active, reserves, or the guard. Being a nineteen-year-old kid, I just needed someone to talk to about it. I was planning to talk to the Marines when I graduated. This recruiter though. He remembered me. He saw me. He asked if we could meet. Easily, I said yes.

Within weeks, I was in the recruiting office with my mom. I told her, "This is happening. I want you to be part of it, but you're not going to talk me out of it."

She didn't fight it. She came.

After the meeting, we walked outside. The sun hit my face, hot and clean, and I felt lighter than I had in months. She looked at me.

"Do you know what today is?"

I shook my head.

"It's the day Jeff died," she said. "Your uncle. My brother. Killed in the Marines."

It was March 12th and we both were quiet. There was nothing else to say.

We just stood there, letting time loop and fold in on itself. Letting the universe remind us that even decisions made in freedom still echo with grief.

Staff Sergeant Duong walked us through the contracts—bonuses, college, service. I skipped infantry. Landed on 13F. Fire Support. Thought it was firefighting. Turns out, I'd be calling in artillery in front of the front lines from a bush in a hill overseeing the battlefield. Eyes in the sky. Voice of God.

Ashley didn't take it well. She cried. Begged. Tried to make me stay.

But I had already said goodbye.

I had asked Travis to go with me and he said, "No I'm good man." Then he made me watch Full Metal Jacket. If you know, you know.

Graduation came. I was the first in my family to walk that stage with a high school diploma—not a GED. Not a dropout. My dad came and when we took a picture together, we look like strangers. We looked like two men who barely knew how to speak to each other. Travis and Ashleigh were there too. Travis was beaming. Ashley was also there with her parents. My family too. It was a moment.

A week later, I left. The night before, the four of us—me, Travis, and both Ashleys—went down to the river. We talked about dreams. About futures. About nothing. It felt like everything.

Earlier that day, I'd gotten into it with Josh. My little brother called Ashley something he shouldn't have, and I snapped. Threw the first punch. He finished it. Left me with a black eye. Real poetic—heading off to basic with a shiner from my fifteen-year-old brother. Travis laughed for hours. "You really gonna let him send you to war looking like that?"

Showing up to basic with a shiner from my fifteen-year-old brother was peak poetic irony. Great first impression for the drill sergeants—'Yeah, you should see the other guy… He's a high school freshman.

We laughed. We talked. And then we all went home, because the world doesn't stop for kids wanting to be soldiers or their families.

I packed my bags. Laid awake. Waited for morning.

Basic stripped me bare. No identity. No phone. Just a uniform and orders.

A month in, I got to make a phone call.

I called Ashley because it had been a couple weeks and no letter. No word. So of course, my heart jumped when she picked up.

She said Travis had been making her uncomfortable. Said he was hitting on her. The moment she said it, it felt like the air left the world.

I called him next. He picked up. Probably mid-shift at Taco Bell.

I asked if it was true.

And instead of denying it—or even explaining—he said, "Why the fuck would you even ask me that?"

When Travis hung up, I stood frozen, receiver heavy in my hand, heart pounding so hard it echoed in my ears. My throat closed around the words I wished I'd said, questions unanswered, choking me in silence.

Just like that.

That was the last time—for a long, long time—that I heard his voice.

16
The Grind

Here's the thing about basic—you're going high speed from the second your boots hit the floor to the moment your head crashes into a pillow. There's no luxury of downtime. No room to sit with your thoughts or untangle your emotions. You don't get to process loss or betrayal. You just move. You go. You execute.

Yeah, you miss people. You miss home. But it comes in flashes— brief gut punches when you get a letter and realize that somewhere out there, someone's still thinking about you. Still writing. Still caring. But even then, you can't hold onto it for long. You're too locked in. Too mission-focused. So you compartmentalize. You shelve it. And you keep going.

Maybe that's why I never processed what happened with Travis. I think I shoved it down and told myself I'd deal with it later. That maybe when I got back, we'd figure it out. I mean, I betrayed our friendship—I know that now. I believed someone else's version of the truth before giving him a real chance to speak his own. And maybe that was the damage. Or maybe it was deeper. But at the time, I didn't know how to fix it. I only knew how to survive.

And basic? That became my rebirth.

I went in chubby. Out of shape. Barely able to clock under 14 minutes on the two-mile run. I failed the PT test twice before finally passing it on the third try—gasping for air, drenched in sweat, but standing. From that point on, I found my rhythm. I leaned into the structure. I liked knowing exactly what the next hour held. The certainty brought clarity. And, weirdly enough, I also loved the moments that interrupted that routine—the curveballs, the fire drills, the chaos that tested who you were when everything went sideways. Because you don't get to raise your hand on a battlefield and say, "Welp, shit outta luck." You adapt. You move. You fix it.

And that mindset? That adaptability? That fast, pressure-driven decision-making? It wasn't new to me. That was survival mode. That was my childhood. That was growing up in a house where you had to read the room like your life depended on it. I had been training for this long before the Army showed up.

I found pride in the smallest things. Cleaning my rifle until it gleamed. Folding my gear just right. Making my locker look like a damn recruiting poster. I had the tightest setup in the bay—efficient, minimal, clean. So clean that eventually, I was the one teaching all 63 guys how to pass inspection. That was my superpower. Organized chaos, refined to precision.

It was an all-male compound. No female soldiers in sight until graduation. And when that day finally came, my mom was there. Ashley and her parents came too. She even brought her friend Shelby. My brothers. My sister. My dad made it by a phone call.

I remember hearing the way my dad talked about me—with pride I hadn't seen or heard before. Like I had finally become something. Like the uniform suddenly made me worthy. Like the boots and the beret and the stripes had filled in whatever blanks he thought I had.

And I remember feeling this twist in my gut. This bitterness I couldn't shake.

Because this? This was mine. My purpose. My promise. Something I committed to when I was thirteen, standing alone in a world that kept gutting me. I fought for this. I bled for this. I built this. And now he wanted to be proud? Not of me—but of the title? The uniform? The story he could now tell his friends at the bar?

That pride wasn't for me. It was for him.

And it made me sick.

Because the people who should've been there were Diane. My grandpa. Travis.

But I didn't let that bitterness consume me. Not fully. Because then I'd look at Ashley, her mom Pam, her dad Dave—and I'd feel something else. Stability. Safety. While my family brought noise and chaos, they brought quiet strength. They showed up like they always did. With warmth. With pride that didn't come with conditions. And it made the moment easier to hold.

After basic came AIT. I finally got my phone back. I could hear Ashley's voice again. Talk to her daily. I reached out to Ashleigh too, trying to find a trace of Travis. She had written me nearly every week during basic—more than anyone else. More than my mom. More than Ashley, even. Just one from my dad. A couple from my mom. But Ashleigh? Consistent. Steady. Her loyalty kept me tethered.

I asked if she'd heard from him. She said not really. And I didn't know if that meant he still needed space from me—or if she was protecting him. I didn't push. I didn't want to know the answer if it hurt.

But the silence ate at me.

We were the three musketeers. We weren't supposed to just drift. Before I left, we said this was temporary. That we'd come back together. That life wouldn't change us. But life doesn't ask for permission.

I texted Travis. No reply.

And I knew then—it was going to take a face-to-face conversation to fix what broke. What I broke.

When I got home, Ashley was starting her senior year of high school. I got us an apartment. She moved in not long after. I used some of my bonus money to buy a car. Ironically, it was her old car—one her parents had been trying to offload. Full circle.

Of course, I added 12-inch subwoofers. Because what's the point of rolling through town if people can't hear you coming from two blocks away?

I was loud back then. In every way.

Still buzzing from that Iron Patriot, post-basic energy, I decided to mark it. Ink it in. So I did what made sense to my 19-year-old brain: I got "AMERICAN" tattooed across my back in bold, block letters.

I told myself I'd earn the right to come back and add "SOLDIER" underneath it after my first deployment.

Ashleigh helped me land a new sales job. I crushed it. I didn't sell phones—I sold belief. People came in needing a solution, and I gave them confidence. It wasn't about manipulating—it was about connecting. Listening. Helping them trust me enough to follow my lead. I wasn't selling— I was leading.

Ashley's senior year was a parade of parties. Our own place. Our own rules. People in and out like a rotating cast of a sitcom. Good shitty drinking food. Cheap liquor. Loud music. Late-night arguments. Makeups. Meltdowns.

Ashleigh crashed at our place once in awhile—sometimes one night, sometimes the whole weekend. Depending on how long the party lasted. Depending on how much life we were trying to escape.

And then it all blew up.

I found out Ashley had
been talking to another
guy. And I lost it.

Not just in a jealous, possessive way. In that bone-deep betrayal kind of way. The kind that makes your stomach drop and your chest tighten all at once. She left—went back to her parents' place after what I'll generously call an intense exchange of words.

Ashleigh showed up not long after. She sat with me while I tried to wrap my head around what the hell had just happened. Just listened. Just stayed. No judgment. No advice. Just presence. And then… Ashley came back.

I listened to her before I took her back. And I wouldn't understand why—not really—until I was thirty-five.

Back then, I just said, "Let's move forward."

Like momentum could save us. Like pretending would make it okay.

Toward the end of her senior year, I was still at the sales job. Still making decent money. But it didn't feel like enough. Not with my grandfather's voice echoing in my head:

Provide. Protect. Be someone they can count on.

Then Ashley told me.

She was pregnant.

At twenty years old I was going to be a father.

A thousand thoughts rushed in. My dad. My grandpa. Dave. Everything they were. Everything they weren't. Everything I could be. Everything I had to be.

I wasn't just surviving for me anymore.

Now I had to survive for someone else.

It was terrifying.

It was thrilling.
It was everything, all at once.

When Ashley walked across her graduation stage, she was pregnant. And I stood there watching her, thinking, "Okay. This is real now. This is happening."

I had to step it up. Where I was wasn't cutting it. One lump sum team commission check a month wasn't enough. I needed more. I put my head down and I found a better job. Better commission. More control.

And then, in December, my son was born.
Kaden Joseph Borchers.

9:09 p.m. December 9th.

It was a long labor being a fight to the finish. I was there the whole time. When they handed him to me—wrinkled, tiny, screaming—I made a promise.

I will be better than my father.

I will be the good I saw in every man who showed up. I will be present. I will be kind. I will guide, not punish. I will teach, not yell. I will love with a fire that never dies. I tattooed his name on my arm, just above a cross.

That bond? Permanent.

Then, just weeks later, we were activated.

Obama's inauguration. The National Guard sent us to D.C. for security.

For three days, I was technically a cop. Sworn in. Deputized. Me—a 21-year-old soldier, father, phone salesman—walking the streets of the nation's capital with laminated credentials and no weapon.

We held checkpoints. Froze our asses off. Watched the motorcade zip by. I like to think he waved.

The streets were packed. Bodies pressed shoulder to shoulder. When the ceremony ended, people flooded the avenues like a tidal wave. Celebration spilled over everything. A sea of hope and history.

And when we came back, it wasn't to a hill to practice calling for fire. Not for me anyways. I was in a branch off unit which put me behind a computer.

Not with the normal unit. Not calling fire missions. Not where I thought I'd be. I was in a cubicle. Comms support. Watching. Waiting. Alone.

That pattern? I knew it.

Isolated after Diane. Alone after my dad. Distant after Travis. And now here again cut off, watching life from a screen. Kaden was growing and I was missing it. Ashley and I weren't good. We tolerated each other. She said I worked too much. I worked less. Then we didn't have money. I worked more. And around and around we went.

But I remembered what Grandpa said:

Take care of your family. Especially the women.

So I put my fucking head down and began to grind.

At twenty-one, I was making more money than some professors. Selling phones. Leading teams. Winning awards.

We were only twenty-one and twenty. A mortgage. A baby. Two cars. One home.

And a relationship held together by obligation and routine instead of love.

Then my mom got married.

Kaden wore this tiny suit—little tie and all. Adorable.

I stood next to her new husband in a tux, watching her glow after I walked her down the aisle.

Then I saw it.

Front row. One chair left empty.

On it? A framed picture of my grandfather.

At the base? His black cowboy boots.

And it hit me like a freight train.

He should've been the one walking her down the aisle.

Instead, it was me.

And I fucking lost it.

Tears poured. Shoulders shook. There was no stopping it.

Because while her new chapter was beginning... mine was already cracking at the seams.

Ashley thought I didn't appreciate her. Thought I couldn't see her.

And maybe I didn't. Not fully.

Because I was still trying to breathe.

I thought she didn't understand how hard I was trying. That this grind was love.

But I wasn't good at the little things. The notes. The flowers. The softness.

I hated small talk. Still do.

I jump straight in. No warm-up. That's something I picked up from Travis. He never said hi. Just launched into it. "You like red? Cool. I like blue. Fuck you."

It stuck.

I didn't realize how much that rubbed her raw. How much she needed those soft moments to feel seen.

So I kept grinding.

She kept feeling invisible.

We kept spinning in opposite directions.

And then...

We found out she was pregnant again.

17

A Needle to the Spine

There I was—twenty-two, or close enough not to matter. A father. A husband. A guardsman in the Iowa Army National Guard. A top performer in sales. From the outside, it looked like I had my shit together. Clean cut. Motivated. Family man. Picture perfect.

Inside?

I was standing on a fucking fault line. Cracks spidering beneath me. Just waiting for the quake.

Ashley and I were already running hot and cold. Neither of us had the tools to fix it. Money fights. Silence. Unspoken resentments. Trying to meet each other's needs when we barely knew our own. I thought I was doing it right. Showing up. Providing. Being present. But no one teaches you how to play husband at twenty-one. Hell, no one had taught me how to be a man. I was winging it. And we were already off the rails before we even knew what direction we were heading.

Then death showed up again—not in the form of someone I loved. Not this time.

This time, it whispered something darker. You're not in control.

And I listened.

It started with a twinge in my lower back. Dull. Annoying. Easy to ignore. I chalked it up to work or training. Figured it was nothing. But within days, that dull ache turned into white-hot agony. I went from limping to crawling. From walking into the house to dragging myself through the front door like I'd just survived a car crash. One night in December, it took me forty-five minutes to get from my car to the couch. Every step was fire—like someone was twisting a hot screw into my spine, pulling nerves tight like guitar strings about to snap.

Ashley checked my temperature—103. She checked again. Still climbing.

"We're going to the ER," she said, no room for argument.

I barely remember the ride. She said I was hallucinating—talking about people who weren't there. Faces in trees. Holding conversations with ghosts. But I remember the hospital. I remember the needle.

Jesus. That needle.

They brought it in like they were setting up an execution. A spinal tap. They told me to curl up in the fetal position, knees to chest, and then they drove that medieval lance into my lower back like they were mining for demons.

It felt like lightning hit my spine.

My whole nervous system lit up—white-hot, then numb, then pure chaos. I saw stars. Heard screaming I wasn't sure was mine.

They hooked me to three IVs—antibiotics, fluids, painkillers that didn't do shit. I lay there in a dark hospital room, cloth over my eyes, lights off, hoping the silence would dull the pain.

It didn't.

The pain hovered like smoke. You never saw it. But it stayed. And it clawed at you.

Diagnosis: meningitis. And spinal cysts—small, cruel things pressing against my nerves. No one knew how it started, but the theory? A bad tooth. A filling I'd ignored. Bacteria leaked into my bloodstream and made itself at home.

The meds burned like acid. They blew through two veins before finding one that didn't feel like fire. Then came the infectious disease doctor.

"We're putting in a PICC line."

I'd never heard of it. But I learned fast. It was a long tube snaked through my arm straight into my heart. One wrong move and the consequences felt biblical.

I spent Christmas in the hospital. New Year's Eve, I got out— barely.

We celebrated at Ashley's parents' place in the country. I couldn't lift Kaden. Could barely lift myself. That PICC line was a wire of fear trailing out of my body. A constant reminder that my health, my future, my control, was hanging by a thread.

Then it came back.

Fever. Pain. Another trip to the ER. They talked about surgery. About cutting out the cysts. My body had started rejecting everything. Medications. IVs. Hope.

They pulled the PICC line. Inserted another one in my opposite arm giving me matching long lasting scars. I was sent home where I was taught how to administer the medicine on my own. We had to fill half our refrigerator with my antibiotic fluid and IV bags. Ashley had started working at a call center. Her mom came by to help. And I sat in the basement like a ghost. Not a father. Not a husband. Just something with a heartbeat and nothing left to give.

No sales. No commissions. FMLA gave me 60% of my income and 0% of my confidence. I thought maybe this near-death experience would pull us closer.

It didn't.

Ashley stayed upstairs. I stayed in the dark. Not out of resentment—but out of shame. I didn't want Kaden to see me like this. Pale. Weak. Tubed up like a science experiment.

So I stayed below. In silence. In pain. In fear.

I missed milestones. First laughs. Smiles. Words. Not all of them—but enough. Enough to make me feel like I was watching my life from behind glass. Close enough to see, but too far to touch.

The pain never fully left. I was prescribed heavy narcotics— oxycodone and the rest of the pharmacy's worst. Looking back, I'm lucky I didn't get hooked. I had the pills. I had the reason. I had the isolation. But something inside me still had fight. I threw them out.

When I was strong enough, I went back to work. I needed it. I needed purpose. A win. Normalcy.

That's when I met him.

Stone.

Ashley had made friends at her new job. One of them was Mike whose nickname was Stone. He was a longtime bodybuilder who had done time in a Mexico prison, and his wife confirmed that. Dude was built like he could throw a couch across a football field. Tattooed head to toe like every scar had been painted on with purpose.

We bonded over ink, fucked up childhoods, and life's toughness. I showed him my tattoos, the ambigrams for my initials combined with my grandpa, one for Kaden, and American across my back. Then I showed him the ambigram on my arm for my parent's initials. I told him the one for my dad got a reaction I wasn't expecting.

I remember my dad saying, "That's stupid. You'll regret it. What if something happens and you never talk to me again? Or you and Kaden fall out?"

That line haunted me.

But Stone got it. He understood why we tattoo names. Why we mark ourselves to hold on to the people we're afraid to lose. He challenged me while poking at my identity. Pushed me to think bigger which all felt familiar, distant, but something I knew and was missing. And maybe I needed that. Maybe I needed someone who wasn't impressed by my medals or my grind.

Ashley encouraged me to spend time with him. Said I needed guy time and even during the week and didn't blink twice when I said we're bar hopping on a Thursday night.

So we drank. We stayed out late. We acted like we were twenty and bulletproof. I wasn't and that wasn't the lifestyle I was ever built for. But I tried.

We even hung out as couples—Stone and his wife, me and Ashley. They were older. A decade, maybe more. But it worked. For a while.

In June, I went in for a routine checkup on my back. Nothing major—just part of the process. A box to check so I could get cleared.

My unit had been activated for a tour in Afghanistan.

This was it. The moment I had waited for. Trained for. Dreamed about since I was thirteen years old, sitting in front of the television, watching those towers fall. That day had carved something into my bones—a sense of duty, of purpose, of who I was supposed to become.

And now it was here. My time. My turn.

But that purpose—my purpose—was ripped from me in a sterile exam room by a man in a lab coat holding a clipboard.

The doctor walked in, barely looking up and calmly erased everything I'd been building toward.

"You're not deployable," he said, as casually as if he were canceling dinner plans.

Those words echoed through me, emptying my chest like a shotgun blast. All the training, all the discipline, all the purpose—gone in an instant, leaving behind only silence and the ghost of a dream I could no longer reach. I felt stripped bare.

"You listening son?" he asked, breaking me out of my trance staring into the void that was torn open where my purpose used to be, "You're not deployable. I can't sign off on you going with your unit."

"I'm not even sure how much use you'll be to the military in the coming years," he added, almost casually.

Looking back, it felt prophetic. Like he was Dr. Strange peering through time, already seeing what I couldn't—that within months of my unit returning, I'd be scrubbed from the roster and honorably discharged. No ceremony. No warning. Just gone. As quick as a spell, my so-called purpose vanished.

And in that present moment—back in that sterile room, grounded in reality—everything I had built my identity around crumbled.

This wasn't just a delay but an erasure. Of my mission. My calling. My entire reason for enduring everything up to that point. All the sacrifice, the struggle, the belief that I was meant for something greater—it vanished in a flood of fluorescent light and bureaucratic indifference.

And in the silence that followed, death smiled.

Sat back in its seat.

And watched as my purpose died that summer of 2010, alone.

Then came July.

It's hard to grieve when you're celebrating life. The universe allowed me 10 minutes to be upset that what I felt I needed to do was gone. I buried the heartache. I shoved an unraveled purpose down deep inside my soul.

Because our daughter, Jersie Lee Borchers, was born on July 3rd, the day after my dad's birthday. Yes, we heard all about how she should have gotten here sooner.

And when she arrived, the doctor pressed her footprints onto my chest, right over my heart, onto the gray shirt I was wearing.

I still have that shirt. Sometimes I still take it out around her birthday.

That night in the hospital, something shifted inside me. As I held her—my Jersie—rocking her in that stiff hospital chair with monitors humming low in the background, this wave hit me. Not just love. Not just pride. Protection. Fierce and primal. The kind of need that curls around your ribcage and never lets go. She was mine. My daughter.

Every word I'd ever heard about protecting women, about what a man should be, came roaring back in echoes. I didn't just feel it—I swore it, sitting there with her tiny body on my chest. I would protect her from this world, no matter what it took. No matter what it cost. I went and had her name tattooed over my heart with her birth flower and would eventually connect it with Kaden's tattoo. Keeping them close forever.

Stone and his wife came to the hospital. Held Jersie. Talked with us. Sat in the room like family. Like nothing was broken.

But something was and my guard was down, so I had no fucking clue.

And then came the unraveling.

One day, I walked into the kitchen. Our two Blackberry phones sat on the counter. Same model. No cases. Just… twins.

I picked one up, thinking it was mine.

The first message:

"Last night was great."

From Mike.

Only in my phone, he was saved as Stone.

I felt my stomach drop. Cold. Heavy.

I scrolled.

And kept scrolling.

Message after message. Day after day. Memory after memory I didn't know had been made— because I wasn't the one making them.

Ashley had let him in. Made him my friend. Let him hold my daughter.

And now, I knew.

Our relationship wasn't drowning.

It had already sunk.

And I had been drifting alone in the wreckage the whole damn time.

18
Symbiotes and Silence

Me and my ex's relationship could've been its own comic saga—twisted arcs, cliffhangers, betrayals, redemption that never quite sticks. But this story? It ain't about that saga. It's about what it did to me. What it turned me into.

Because after the betrayal, after I found out, I didn't just feel pain—I felt possession.

Like something had latched onto me. Something dark. Like one of the black, swirling alien symbiotes from the comics I grew up on. You don't notice it at first. It creeps in. Wraps itself around your nervous system. Merges with your voice, your skin, your thoughts. And then one day, you look in the mirror and you're still you—but not. Your reflection blinks back at you with sharper teeth. A colder stare. A silence you don't remember building.

That's what heartbreak did to me. That's what betrayal was—a fucking symbiote. Not loud. Not violent. Just patient and parasitic. Feeding off the version of me that used to believe in something good. And I hated her for it. Hated that she walked away like she didn't leave venom in my veins.

It took years to even begin unpacking it. Not because some therapist sat me down and gave me permission to feel. Not because some divine sign beamed down and told me I was enough.

I just… got it one day. It clicked.

But back then?

My life had become chaos theory in practice—one betrayal creating ripples, ripples becoming waves, waves reshaping everything I thought was stable.

Back then, I was chaos.

Pure fucking chaos. No clarity. No compass. No sense of what was up, who to trust, or how to breathe. And in the middle of all that emotional rubble, I did something that felt impossible—I stood up. I spoke. Not to lash out or burn it all down, but to use my voice the way people like Diane and my grandpa had shown me. I needed someone who knew me—before the pain, before the marriage, before the silence took hold.

I had nowhere else to turn. Nobody I trusted to lean on. I sure as hell wasn't going to dump my soul out to some work buddy who didn't really know me. Travis was the only one I could even maybe turn to. And yeah, maybe I deserved to get swung on. Maybe he'd put me on my ass. But fuck it—at least that would've been something. Better than the nothing I was carrying.

He was bartending at this spot in town. I walked into the spot he was at with my heart jackhammering against my ribs, not knowing if I'd find forgiveness or a fist. But Travis just nodded, like the past didn't matter. Like he'd been waiting for this moment as much as I had.

The same nod he gave me the very first time we met. Like he was saying: "Yeah. You're good. You can stay."

I slid onto the stool.

"Dan, how's it going?"

"How are you, Trav?" I asked, my voice steadier than I felt.

"What brings you by?" he said, like I wasn't clearly running on fumes and desperation.

"I need a drink."

"Dealer's choice," I added.

That smirk widened. "Say less."

He handed me his twisted version of a Long Island Iced Tea. After two of those, I was buzzed deep enough to feel my shoulders drop for the first time in months. He didn't press me. Just moved around the bar like he always did—half bartender, half therapist, all heart.

He had this gift. The way he saw people. Not just their stories, but their weight. Their trauma. He took your burden and carried it like it was his own. That night, he didn't judge. Didn't shit-talk Ashley. Didn't ask why I didn't call sooner. He just asked about me. About Kaden. About Jersie. About where my head really was.

Later, we stepped outside for a smoke. Cold air wrapped around us, sharp and quiet. Between drags and laughter, he suddenly grinned and said, "Hey, remember when I had weed in my pocket and you didn't know I had two phones?"

I almost choked. "Oh my God, yes! I was scared shitless when the cop said, 'What's this?' and you go, 'It's my phone.'"

Travis leaned back against the wall, eyes sparkling. "Yeah—and you looked over at the phone already on the hood like you were about to shit a brick."

"Bro!" I gasped, laughing so hard my eyes teared up. "Why the hell did you have two phones at seventeen?!"

He gave me that signature Travis smirk. "Because I piss excellence, Dan."

We roared. Loud. Reckless. Full-bellied laughter that cracked something open in me. That kind of laughter only shows up when you feel safe again for the first time in a long time.

I remembered every beat of that night we'd laughed about. We had just picked up a car—new to me, dealer plates still on. I forgot the insurance card, of course. Classic move. It was past curfew. We cut off a cop at midnight. Flashing lights. Pulled over fast.

Travis told me earlier that night he had weed in his pocket.

The cop reached into his jacket, felt a bump. The cop asked, "What's this?"

"My phone," Travis answered.

Then the cop patted his other pocket and said, "Yeah? What's in this one?"

I nearly died in that moment.

But the cop reached in and when he pulled his hand out, another fucking phone.

They let us go. Told us to park the car until we got plates and proof. No ticket. No lecture. Just a warning.

We did what any dumb, lucky teenagers would do.

We hit La Juanita's like nothing happened. Two burritos each and a large pineapple juice a piece. We laughed in my apartment that night until we couldn't breathe. We were damn near kings.

That night outside the bar, we talked about Josh and Nate. "They still running around together?" he asked.

I nodded. "Yeah. They're carving out their own legends now."

It was true. They reminded me of us. Inseparable. Brothers. Untouchable in that way only kids with fire in their bones can be.

We talked late into the night—and the nights that followed. Stories. Memories. The future. For those three days, we were legends again.

I told him everything—basic, the Guard, meningitis, the PICC lines, the fear. He told me about a girl he was seeing. About wanting out of Sioux City. About building something that mattered. I told him how his obsession with data and patterns had become my secret weapon. How I used it in sales, reading CEO calls, watching the numbers, staying ten steps ahead because of how he taught me to think.

But that last night—that one etched itself into me.

I got overly drunk. One more of his Long Islands and I'd have blacked out. Needless to say, I couldn't walk or see straight. And Travis—without a second thought—climbed into my F-350, a truck he had never driven, and got me home. He had no idea how to handle something that big, but he figured it out. Steered me home like he was navigating a damn GTA side quest.

Thinking about it, only Travis could turn being a designated driver cruising in an oversized F350 through town into a rescue mission worthy of an action flick. He drove that thing like he stole it—or maybe like he wished he had.

Before I stumbled through the front door of my uncle's house, he said, "It's always about the kids, Dan. That's the only thing that matters. You give them better than what we had."

And that was it.

That line snapped something back into place.

The next day, I called Ashley. Told her we had to figure our shit out. And we tried. We did therapy. Got engaged. I buried myself in work. Moved up. Ran a store. Built a team. Used every tool I had—my grandpa's grit, Travis's brain, Diane's compassion. I became the guy people relied on. The one who got shit done.

At work, I finally broke through. Made it into leadership. Assistant manager. It meant commuting an hour each way, every day. But I didn't care. It was a step. And I was ready.

Six months later, I transferred back to Sioux City. Ten minutes from home. No more cracked windshields and sunrises behind the wheel. I was close. I was climbing. I earned my own store not long after. My name. My team. My people.

And I fucking loved it.

I fell in love with leadership—not just the title. The people. Watching them grow. Watching them make more money. Believe in themselves. Chase something bigger. I didn't need the spotlight—I wanted them to win. Watching others rise became my fire.

Ashley was doing daycare from home at that point. She even watched Ashleigh's little boy. That connection mattered. That bridge stayed strong. Me and Trav. Me and Ashleigh. Ashleigh and Trav. Still showing up in each other's lives.

Ashleigh and Eric, Eric was someone we first met working night shifts at Taco Bell. They had their first little boy then. Travis had a daughter with the girl he had been seeing and named her Magdalena. And for a while, everything felt full circle. Like life had found rhythm. Like the scars had stitched into something solid.

But even when life feels full…

Death knows how to whisper, I'm still here.

I was working one morning, barely twenty minutes into my shift, when my phone buzzed.

Jennifer. My cousin on my dad's side. We didn't talk often. Not like this. Something was wrong.

"There was an accident," she said.

My chest tightened.

"Ant's okay," she added quickly. "He made it out."

Relief. Sharp. Immediate. Then—

"But there were others in the car."

Torey was driving.

"Torey?" I asked. "Like Torey and Matt?"

"Yeah... Matt was in the car. And Dom. Alex too."

"Wait—Alex? James' little brother?"

Another pause. Then:

"Only Ant and Alex made it out."

Just one second. That's all it took. A stream, a flipped car, and everything was gone. Torey. Matt. Dom.

It felt like someone had kicked my lungs out from under me. One phone call, one sentence, and the entire fabric of our history unraveled. I kept seeing their faces—Torey's easy laugh and Matt's confident grin—all wiped away in a blink. It wasn't fair. It wasn't fucking fair.

I hung up and just sat in my office staring at the wall with tears streaming down my face.

Staring at nothing. Hearing everything. Every summer night. Every inside joke. Every ride. Every moment that used to feel invincible.

It hit me harder than I expected—Matt and Torey were gone. And though I didn't know Dom personally like I knew Matt or Torey, it was clear I'd missed out on knowing someone truly great. It was one of those brutal reminders of how fragile time really is—and how quickly we can run out of it.

The realization of them being gone hit when I was at the funerals. Just… gone. I never got to say goodbye. No final words. No last laugh. Just silence where they used to be. And standing there, trying to process that loss, all I could think about was my cousin. What he must've been feeling. What it meant to lose people that close, that young.

Grief doesn't play fair, and it sure as hell doesn't give you time to prepare. Dimitri was there too, carrying his own weight of it—quiet, heavy, and all over his face. We were all just standing in the wreckage, trying to make sense of it. I think that's what made it hurt worse. Not just losing them. But seeing the ones I loved get hit with the same kind of pain I knew too well.

You don't walk away from something like that unchanged.

And you don't always feel lucky. You feel punished.

Yet even in grief, life moved forward—wedding plans, new chapters. But I couldn't step into mine without Travis. Weddings aren't just about who shows up—they're about who isn't there. And there was no way I was letting Travis become another ghost in my story.

I did what Diane had taught me.

I used my voice. Standing on the edge of another milestone, there was only one person I needed beside me—the one who'd always shown up, even when everything else fell apart. I reached for my phone, heart racing again, knowing I had to try. Because weddings are about who's there, sure—but they're also about who's missing. And I refused to let Travis be a ghost.

19
Marked as Coming

The message I sent to Travis that spring was simple:

"Hey man, I'd love it if you could come."

He replied, told me he was engaged too. Said to go ahead and send the invite. Dropped me the address. So, I did.

But it came back: undeliverable.

I messaged him again. Told him the invite got returned. Gave him the date. The location. Everything.
No reply.

So I made the only choice I could: I marked him down as coming.

And then I got back to work.

The rest of that spring—and the summer that followed—was a blur. But not the kind that fades from memory. The kind that builds something. Brick by brick. Fire by fire. I was running hard. Managing a store. Still trying to be a present dad. I was juggling fire with one hand and trying to shake hands with the other.

That's when Kiley transferred into my store from Omaha.

She came in with her fiancé, looking for a fresh start in Sioux City, and I brought her onto my team. From day one, I saw it—

she had that thing you can't teach. The spark. The hunger. The ability to take feedback and turn it into growth like she was wired for it. She didn't just execute. She understood.

Before long, she was killing it.

And then we got selected to represent our company at a national sales role-play competition. I was in the middle of wedding planning, but suddenly I was flying to Nashville as her coach.

We placed second in the nation.

Not the region. Not the division. The entire damn country.

That one moment lit a fire under both our names. Suddenly, my store wasn't just part of the map—it was the one people were watching. And with that attention came access. My director started spending more time around the store. Mentorship. Trust. Insight. Eyes on me.

Then, an opening.

District manager. Grand Island, Nebraska.

I applied.

One month before the wedding.

But we'll come back to that.
Around the same time, I met Mark.

Store manager from Rapid City. Newly dropped into our district. And he didn't like me—at all. Probably thought I was cocky.

Too confident. Too loud. I was on fire, smashing numbers, and our boss made him come shadow me.

He was pissed.

But then he saw how I coached. How I worked. How I poured into my team. He realized I wasn't trying to flex—I was trying to help.

That night, we hit a bar.

And that's when Ashley showed up at Red Robin. Kids in the car. Screaming at me from the parking lot to get home. No warning. No text. Just a full-blown public meltdown in front of my team and a guy I'd just met.

Great first impression.

Oddly enough, that moment broke something open. The tension between me and Mark softened.

The rivalry shifted into respect. Over time, it became something else, friendship. Real friendship. Texts. Calls. Strategy. Wins and losses. Iron sharpening iron. In a life filled with so many silences, Mark became a voice that actually stuck around—a reminder that even the harshest beginnings can soften into something you trust.

By the time August rolled around, the wedding was in motion.

Friends from work were coming. My dad was showing up. Ashleigh was standing beside Ashley in a bridesmaid's dress.

But the spot I'd marked "Travis"?

Stayed empty.

And I'm not gonna lie—everything else looked great. The wedding was beautiful. Music hit. The drinks flowed. The photos came back clean. But this book? It's not about clean.

It's about grief—and the quiet ache of being left behind. That empty chair felt heavier than any presence could've been a ghost haunting the edges of my joy. It wasn't just an absence—it was a silence that echoed through the night, a reminder of something unfinished and lost.

My dad was there that night, but there was no big reunion. No moment where time froze and we hugged it out. We hadn't spoken in three years—not since I got into that late-night car wreck after one of my first assistant manager shifts. I was twenty-two. Dead tired. Driving home on fumes. My fault.

He called to scold me. Like we were back in Rapid. Like I was still a scared kid trying to win his approval.

And I snapped.

Told him he didn't get to show up now. Not after basic. Not after marriage. Not after kids. Not after I had already built a life without him.

We didn't talk again until the wedding.

But still... I invited him.

Because I always do. I always hope.

That maybe if I do the right thing long enough, someone will finally do right by me.

His side of the family came too. That side doesn't always show up, but this time, they did. And Ant came. Just seeing him there was a relief. A weight off my chest. We danced. Laughed. Celebrated like we hadn't been scattered. It was one of those rare times where it felt like we were in the same place—not just physically, but emotionally.

After the reception, a bunch of us rolled out into downtown Sioux City. Still in full wedding gear.

Mark and his date. Ashleigh. My brothers, Bobby and Josh. We took over the night. Bar hopping. Clinking glasses. Letting the celebration bleed out into the streets. Chaos, in the best way. No timelines. No expectations. Just music and motion and the kind of happiness you earn.

But want to hear something weird?

My dad didn't come with us.

Didn't hang back with his side. Didn't grab a drink with me. Didn't toast to his son's wedding. He went bar hopping alone. Just… wandered from place to place. While Jerry, his girlfriend, stayed back at the hotel, he wandered through downtown telling strangers his son got married that day.

He celebrated me—without me. It was the perfect summary of our entire relationship: Always circling. Always missing. Close enough to hurt, but never enough to heal.

That wedding marked more than just a ceremony.

It was my last day in the role I was in.

The following week, I started a new job. I got the district manager position. My first multi-unit leadership role. At twenty-five years old, I was responsible for eighty-five employees across the state of Nebraska.

And in some twisted way, that was the bargain. She got the wedding, the cake, the dress, the moment. And I got the agreement to move. Three and a half hours from everything we'd ever known.

And for me? That was the win.

Because that's what Travis meant when he said to build something better than what we had.

Kaden and Jersie had married parents. A roof over their heads. A future. Disposable income. And if we needed a date night or wanted to take them to the zoo in Omaha? It was an hour and a half away.

I didn't care about the miles. Driving was easy. Life was hard.

Head down, focused, I ran. Fast. Hard. Nonstop. Maybe if I ran hard enough, built big enough, won enough—I could drown out the quiet ache of what I couldn't fix at home. Maybe numbers could silence the whispers of everything that felt empty inside.

My family was scattered across the map like broken glass.

And then, in the middle of all the motion—right when I thought I'd finally hit a stride—I got blindsided.

My dad got cancer.

And just like that—when I thought I'd built enough armor around myself—life swung back harder. My foundation-built brick by brick, suddenly felt fragile again. Ready to crumble beneath my feet.

20
Loyalty, Lifted

Fucking cancer.

My dad was diagnosed with stage 4 melanoma—skin cancer. Just like that, everything cold and distant between us got shoved under a spotlight I never asked for. All the silence, all the space, none of it mattered when death walked in and took a seat like it owned the place.

We started talking again. Cautiously at first, short conversations testing waters long frozen. I checked in almost daily, and for a while, something genuine seemed to form. I told him he was strong, reminded him of his progress, the way he was defying the odds. He sounded hopeful— even grateful. But slowly, the tone shifted.

"Come to Rapid. Bring the grandkids," he'd say, as if I could just drop everything and drive away from the life I was barely managing.

Then came the guilt.

"I could be dead in a month!"

I'd remind him of the doctors' optimism, his resilience, the facts he kept overlooking. But guilt doesn't listen to logic.

Then came the money.
"Buy this off me."
"Pay me back for your wedding gift."

"You owe me."

I started setting boundaries. That's when he did what men like him do when control slips away— he got vicious.

He took it public. Tagged me on Facebook, ranting that he should've beaten my ass more as a kid. His cancer support group rallied around him like a prophet suffering injustice, and suddenly strangers online branded me selfish. Ungrateful. Worthless. Undeserving.

I said the only thing I had left:

"You would've had to be in my life to beat my ass in the first place."

He blocked me. But the voicemails, texts, and calls kept pouring in—rage spilling onto my gay brother with slurs, onto my mom calling her a whore, onto my sister, Josh—people who had nothing to do with his war.

That was it.

I called him one final time. "Congratulations on your remission," I said, and that became the last sentence I ever spoke to my father.

It didn't end with tears. It ended exactly how everything he touched did—bitter, loud, and final.

Then, it was just us. Me, Ashley, and the kids.

Except—at first—it wasn't even that.

I moved to Nebraska alone, spending three months in an empty apartment while Ashley and the kids stayed back to sell the house. Weekends became 48-hour sprints of catch-up before driving back to Grand Island, collapsing onto an air mattress beside a barely functional TV.

Isolation set in quickly, rotting something inside me. I'd seen this pattern before—after my grandpa died, after basic training, after the PICC line. The same rhythm every time: isolation, silence, the slipping.

When Ashley and the kids finally moved down, I tried grounding myself, tried resetting. I poured everything I had into not becoming my dad, into being better than my grandfather.

For a moment, it seemed to work.

We strengthened our marriage. Grew closer. Appreciated each other again.

Just kidding.
We didn't even last a year before it started to unravel again.

Ashley and the kids hadn't fully moved yet—still weekends and visits, pieces of a life boxed up. I thought we were building something noble, sacrificing for the future. Then I found out she was talking to someone else. Again.

Here we fucking go.

She admitted it casually, told her sister, "I love Danny...but I'm not in love with him," as though I were an old sweatshirt she'd worn out of guilt. Meanwhile, I'd been loyal—no booze, no parties, no friends, just family and work. And none of it mattered.

We fought—not loudly, but hollowly. Ashley packed up, took the kids, and went back to her parents in Sioux City. Then came the second gut punch: her sister was mad—not at Ashley for breaking our vows, but because Ashley had hurt the other guy. Her parents said nothing. No one said a word. Not even to defend me. Nobody told Ashley she'd ripped apart something sacred.

I stood alone in the wreckage. No backup. No allies. Just silence.

And in that silence, I felt like the dumbest son of a bitch alive.

Yet still—I let her come back.

Some broken part of me still believed commitment meant something. Still believed if I just improved myself, maybe things would fall into place. So I vowed to love the man in the mirror, to reclaim myself, not for her but for me.

If solitude was the cost, so be it.

I picked up the weights and began to build.

At over 300 pounds, trapped in a body that felt like a cage, I dove into YouTube tutorials, gym advice, macro counting like KPIs. Keto, Strongman, CrossFit, military HIIT, long-distance running—I got obsessed. Cardio became therapy; weightlifting became prayer.

I lost 120 pounds, rebuilt every inch of myself. Not just physically, but mentally, emotionally.

The kid from the '90s with neon dreams? Gone. The soldier, the groom, the man who chased peace? Gone too. If you knew me one year and saw me the next, you wouldn't recognize me— not just my body, but my presence, my conviction, my voice. Even Mark noticed, making comments about how my energy had changed. My advice had teeth now, clarity sharpened by fire.

Then Kiley reached out, needing a job reference. We caught up—fitness, life, laughter. Something solid, genuine, human. She saw me—not obligation, just recognition.

I became a fitness coach on the side—not for money, but for fire, discipline, distraction. When you've been told, "No one else will want you," that lie echoes—until it doesn't. Isolation was something I knew intimately; I'd learned to speak its language long ago. The Bane quote rang true:

"You think the darkness is your ally. But you merely adopted it. I was born in it. Molded by it."

That was me. I didn't just survive darkness; I thrived in it.

One day, a woman smiled at me—nothing romantic, just recognition. It shifted something inside me. Being invisible for years, all it took was one look to remind me: you're still alive.

That night, I confronted Ashley. "How were you able to tell so many other guys you loved them—and tell me you loved me at the same time?"

We fought. She begged. But my mind was made up.

Watching my kids grieve broke me hardest. Kaden was old enough to cry harder when I left; Jersie sensed it too. Their pain lodged in my chest, in my throat every Sunday night as I kissed them goodbye.

They didn't understand that I knew their grief intimately.

It planted a seed of self-hatred within me: You failed them.

One night, in the echoing emptiness of the house, I didn't want comfort or fixing. I just wanted my brother.

I sat down, pulled out my phone, and messaged the only person who'd truly understand.

Travis.

21

Kingborch

I sat there on that worn couch, in a house stripped of everything but the echoes of what used to be, and I finally did what I should've done years ago.

I texted my brother.

My message to Travis:

Hey bro, I know I've said this a few times, but this time it has a different meaning. I put Ashley in front of our friendship. I know you say it's no big deal every time I bring it up—but it was. We're brothers. I should've never turned my back on you for her. And for the last few years, I've been destroyed for choosing her over our friendship. Whether you care or not, I finally grew a pair and said enough is enough. I walked away. I've learned a lot, and one of the most important lessons is this: you should never have to cut your friends out. I finally have freedom. And relief. And at the same time? Guilt. Guilt for the friends and family she made me lose along the way. But you—you were the worst one to lose. It's eaten me alive for years. And I always came to you when she fucked up. Because unlike me, you always stayed true to our friendship. So again, man... I'm sorry.

His reply? Straight soul balm.

Dan, it's all good, man. I was gonna get ahold of you 'cause I saw what was going on, but I figured you might need some space. Everyone probably bombarded you about it anyway. I still consider you a good friend. We can hang out anytime you want, bro. I know in the past I may have said to leave her, but we're fathers now. I hope you guys can rebuild one day—or at least still be friends. I haven't been with my ex for about a year now. We hate each other now. It's not what I want for you. Hope all is well. In the end, if you need to talk or hang out—I'll be here.

That was Travis. Always.

My response:

Thanks, man. I did get bombarded—but this? This was my choice. I walked away. Ashley did the same thing, bro, so I know your anger too well. For our kids' sake, I'm sure we'll figure it out eventually, but dude—I've never been this fucking happy outside of the day my kids were born.

He hit me back:

It's all about the kids. I get my daughter half the time now. It was hard at first because I didn't know how to act around her through all of it... but our relationship's never been better. So I don't let that other shit bother me anymore.

I texted back:

That's reassuring... because I'm scared as fuck about losing my kids. They're everything. And now we're going to be three hours apart. Kaden's asking so many questions. It's tough. But what you said—that helps. It really does.

He kept it simple:

Hit me up when you're in town, bro. Miss you.

That was the moment. The closure I didn't even know I needed.

The next few months were all about momentum.

I kept grinding. Kept lifting. Kept rewiring. I was still young—twenty-six, twenty-seven—but I'd already lived enough chapters for several lifetimes. I didn't have a college phase—I had life. And I used it. Every scar, every silence, every win and wrecked moment became fuel.

Weekends were for my kids. And since my grandma had moved back to Sioux City, I made sure we saw her every visit. Her health was fading—voice softer, steps slower. It was like watching a candle burn low in a dark room, steady then sputtering, desperately memorizing every flicker.

Work began to stall. I was still hitting goals, but it didn't challenge me anymore. Comfort crept in like rot. I needed something more.

I began to open up my circle—met new people, reconnected with Travis, tried breaking free of routine. Then, randomly, I started an Instagram account.

At first, it was about fitness. But soon I posted a meme about pre-workout disasters, and it hit. I posted another. Then another. Suddenly, memes were going viral, and Kingborch was born—an accidental brand built on sweat, sarcasm, and screenshots.

The page exploded. Followers grew—10,000. 15,000. 25,000. I was building a community— voices from across the world sharing jokes, struggles, and wins. People reached out not for clout, but genuine connection. For the first time in years, isolation lifted.
Meanwhile, life shifted again. A new job opened closer to the kids, closer to Travis. I moved to Sioux Falls, leaving retail

behind for medium-sized business sales—a complete pivot, fresh and sharp.

I reconnected with Ashleigh and Travis. Josh and Nate remained unbreakable. Friendships felt authentic again—easy, unforced, real. Even Kiley in Omaha became a familiar, comfortable presence without expectation.

I started socializing, hitting bars and game nights, trying to rediscover who I was without labels. But even that felt fragile, shaped by other voices.

"You're not good at being single—you should be with someone," someone said.

How the fuck does me being in a relationship define who I am as a person?

I'd worked too hard reclaiming myself. So, craving perspective, I booked twenty-one days in Europe. No itinerary, just me and a backpack.

But right before leaving, I posted a meme about late-night pre-workout-induced insomnia. A woman named Melissa commented—clever, playful, sharp. We joked publicly, then privately. Something about our conversation felt easy, genuine. Intriguing.

The next day, I boarded a plane to Europe, not knowing the wingman for my next chapter waited on the other side of a meme.

22

Across the Pond, Beyond the Past

For a while now, I'd been holding my relationship with my kids together through a patchwork of FaceTime calls, weekend visits, hotel stays, and whatever weekday drop-ins I could manage. I did everything I could to stay involved—despite the distance, the custody schedule, the chaos. And now that I was living just an hour away, it made things easier. At least logistically.

But time? Time's an unpredictable bastard.

They were growing—fast. Their lives filling up with school, sports, activities. Even being closer didn't mean I always got to see them more. Their calendars were as booked as mine. But I stayed close. I stayed consistent. We were making it work. Even if it wasn't always perfect.

Life outside of fatherhood had started shifting, too.

I found a new rhythm through work. Built a solid friend group. Mark became a close one—sharp guy, and we had some great debates. The kind that didn't end with one of us pissed off, just thinking deeper. Kiley and I kept in touch. Our friendship was this strange little life-coaching loop. I talked her through her relationship chaos; she gave me honesty I could actually use. She was solid. Ashleigh—who I had always called my little sister—still checked in from time to time. Just enough to remind me that not all bonds break. Some just stretch.

And then?

I got on a plane.

First stop: Dublin.

Twenty-one days across Europe. No work emails. No morning meetings. No kids knocking on my door. Just me, a passport, and a phone full of fitness memes and strangers I'd somehow turned into friends.

Night two in Dublin, I finally met up with someone from the original meme Instagram group that we had been in for years. We had joked, tagged each other, built this weird online rhythm.

And now we were walking cobblestone streets until 3 a.m., barhopping, laughing, learning how Dublin got down. I made it back to the hotel without a working phone, half-drunk in a foreign city I didn't fully understand. To this day, I don't know how I didn't end up face-down in a canal.

But man—I was alive.

Also, on that phone? Melissa.

We were still messaging. Back and forth. Swapping stories as I bounced from city to city. I'd tell her what I was seeing. The people I was meeting. Where I was headed next. It wasn't flirty. It wasn't heavy. It was just… easy.

From Ireland, I hopped to London.

That's where I met Kashy—one of the OG meme creators I'd known since we both had under a hundred followers. She was at half a million now, but the clout didn't matter. We weren't in it for followers. We were in it to make people laugh. To connect. To cut through the bullshit with humor.

Meeting her in person was wild. We were both introverts—shy, awkward at first. But we'd known each other online for years. Voice notes. Memes. Divorce talk. Gym talk. Real talk. I crashed on her couch. She showed me around London in the in-between hours of her job. It wasn't flashy. It wasn't curated. It was just two people who had seen each other through screens... now sharing the same city.

I rode the London Eye. Watched the city stretch like a living map under glass. I made the pilgrimage to the Harry Potter set— saw the props, walked the halls where childhood met magic. And for the first time in a long time, I felt something close to wonder. Not because I believed in wands and wizards. But because I finally believed in escape.

By then, Melissa and I had moved from Instagram to Snapchat. Swapping updates. Pictures. Voice notes. Jokes. She'd never been to Italy—despite being Italian—which, obviously, gave me ammo. I promised to send photos from Rome just to mess with her.

London gave way to Paris.

I took the long route. No rush. No one waiting. Just me, my bag, and a mind wide open.

In Paris, I went to the Eiffel Tower. Bought a glass of champagne and drank it alone at the top, looking out at the city like it belonged to no one and everyone all at once. No texts to reply to. No partner to check in with. Just peace. Just height. Just me.

But not everything glittered.

I walked the catacombs—down, deep beneath the city. Past walls lined with skulls. Royals. Peasants. Soldiers. Children. Stacked bone on bone, no names, no titles. Just human remains.

Dead is dead.

And still, it didn't feel grim. It felt honest. Like truth with no costume. Equal. Necessary.

Then came Italy.

Rome was heat and history. The Vatican, intense. The Mona Lisa—smaller than I expected, but magnetic. Still, it was the Coliseum that stuck with me. I stood there, in the shadow of a monument to blood and spectacle. Men fought there—not for glory, but for survival. For someone else's entertainment. History calls them warriors. Movies call them heroes.

But what I saw were victims of a system. Glamorized suffering. Sacrifice wrapped in applause.

And still—it moved me.

My Airbnb sat right across the street. Every morning, I'd wake to sunlight cresting over that broken stone monument. Light would hit my window in a way that felt intentional. Like something divine was trying to tap me on the shoulder.

It reminded me of Travis.

His sentimental ass. The way he'd whisper, "The moon's beautiful tonight," like he was talking to God and expecting a reply. He always found the beauty I missed. Felt the world deep.

And in those mornings, I felt him.

Even a world away—I felt connected.

So yeah, I took pictures. And yeah, I teased Melissa—because I couldn't help but remind her of one simple fact: she was Italian … and I was in Italy.

She'd never been.

I leaned all the way into it, sending snaps from cobblestone streets and sun-soaked piazzas, playing it up just enough to make her laugh.

Then Snapchat crashed.

No hesitation—we traded numbers.

"Let's not lose this," I said.

And we didn't.

That same night, she said she had a date. I told her to go for it. Cheered her on. She told me I should talk to someone too. Said I was in Europe—live a little. I told her I'd never had a one night stand. Never hit on someone at a bar. She said, "You're in Europe. You gotta live a little."

Challenge accepted.

Venice.
I was sitting riverside at a café, cigarette in hand, sipping coffee.
A woman sat a few seats away—German, studying in Canada,
traveling solo. Cool energy. I texted the guy I was with for
backup. He showed up… wearing the same color shirt as me.

I texted Melissa: "Dude showed up looking like my reflection."
She laughed. Egged me on.

Somehow, it turned into a conversation. The woman sat with us.
Talked. Laughed.

Then my buddy—whose mom I happened to work with—said,
"Hey, if you come back to the Airbnb, you can meet my mom."

She dipped. Fast.

I told Melissa everything the next day. She was howling.

Her date? Just as bad.

We laughed. Swapped stories. Shared memes. Shared pieces of
ourselves.

Rome. Venice. Then back to London. Kashy's couch again. Then
Sweden. Then home.

When I landed in Minneapolis and drove back to Sioux Falls,
Melissa messaged:

"I live in Chicago. If you're ever out this way, swing by. Let's
grab lunch."

Perfect timing.

Brian—one of the first meme creators I ever connected with—lived in Chicago too. I hit him up. Told him I might come through.

He said, "Hell yeah."

I planned a trip to Chicago.

I was going to meet Melissa.
Finally.

Meet Brian.
Finally.
Another chapter, born from strangers and memes and the version of me I'd fought like hell to become.

By then, work had taken another leap. Associate Director. Four-state territory. Business channel.

Lifting. Climbing. Building momentum. The version of me Melissa was about to meet?

He was steady. Driven.
Full of rhythm.
Full of purpose.
Confident in the chaos.

But what neither of us knew—
What I didn't know—
Was that the man she met that day?

He wouldn't survive what was coming next.

23
11:11

"We are all made of star stuff." – Carl Sagan

They say 11:11 is a sign.

A divine alignment. A cosmic wink from a universe that's finally paying attention. Some call it an angel number, others a glitch in the matrix. It's the whisper from the other side, a brief moment when reality and magic brush fingertips.

Make a wish, they say.

But I didn't make a wish on November 11. I just showed up.

That was the day I met Melissa. 11/11. We joked later that the date was too symbolic to ignore, as if the universe penciled us into its calendar. But in that moment, sitting across from her, I wasn't thinking about signs or cosmic alignments. I was just trying to remember how to breathe. Because I couldn't speak.

Not at first.

Melissa filled every silence effortlessly—her words flowing like water over river stones, smooth and constant, revealing stories about growing up, heartaches, laughter, and those peculiar details that made us eerily similar. We both carried our mothers' last names, shared near-identical eye colors, and each had a single dimple—but on opposite sides. Coincidences stacked high enough that I wondered if the universe was playing some kind of intricate joke.

I just sat there, quiet, soaking it in. Soaking her in.

She leaned in at one point, eyes bright with amusement. "You just traveled across Europe, and you've got nothing to say?"

I chuckled nervously. "Apparently jet lag hits the vocal cords first."

Her laugh broke the ice completely.

Later that evening, we went for a drive. The car hummed beneath us as we moved through the soft wash of the universe's evening light—stars above, shadows stretching long across the road. And somewhere between the quiet and the motion, I finally found my voice.

"Is this what you thought I'd be like?" I asked.

She smiled, turning toward me, her face calm in the starlight. "Honestly? You're so much quieter than I expected."

I let out a breath. "Sometimes I surprise myself," I said, realizing even as the words left my mouth that something in me had already started to crack open.

By the next day, the words came easier. We explored the city like we'd always been part of it— steps falling into rhythm, conversations flowing with ease. And then, walking side by side beneath the glow of towering manmade light—all steel and glass and movement—I reached over and took her hand. No hesitation. No second-guessing.

Just fingers that found each other like magnets finally allowed to meet. A quiet fell over us in the big and loud city. It wasn't silence. It wasn't awkwardness. It was peace—the rare, profound kind I'd only heard about in whispers.

When it was time to leave, she didn't just wave goodbye. Melissa cried. A real, heartbroken cry that tore right through me. It wasn't just friendship anymore, and we both knew it.

But reality was waiting. Eight hours away. Back to work, back to juggling parenting schedules, back to video calls and the distance that tested every promise we'd quietly begun to make.

Thanksgiving came, and Melissa reached out: "Spend it with my family… if that's not too weird."

Family. The word hit deep. She knew my story—she knew how I'd chased that concept all my life, like a dog after a car, not sure what I'd do if I ever caught it.

I went.

Melissa's family was warm, real, messy—the kind I'd always dreamed of being part of. Her granny took my hand, eyes twinkling mischievously. "Isn't she amazing?" She asked it rhetorically, a declaration rather than a question. Melissa checked on me often, grounding me in rooms full of unfamiliar faces, never letting me float too far from her orbit.

By January, we'd found ourselves deeply in love.

Not the reckless, adolescent kind. Something slower, richer— like a star forming out of cosmic dust, gradually building mass until it ignites. Real. Earned. Honest.

Our dates were orchestrated chaos—flights, long drives, and hotel rooms filled with laughter, exhaustion, and takeout containers. I flew her in, drove her home, every goodbye a little harder, every reunion a little brighter.

Then life threw a curveball: Melissa lost her job. I saw the fear flicker behind her eyes. Bills, rent, uncertainty. Without hesitation, I told her, "We're fine. Handle your world, I've got us covered."

Eventually, I relocated to Chicago—another bold pivot, another leap into the unknown. Our first year together was electric. Melissa introduced me to EDM, concerts, festivals—a symphony of sound and light that became our shared heartbeat. We danced until sunrise, collapsing into each other's laughter, wrapped in the aftermath of pure adrenaline.

Our love wasn't just romance—it was quirky, offbeat, and uniquely ours. We had Tim, our Squishmallow companion, who somehow found himself joining every laser fueled EDM adventure to quiet nights on the couch; he became our constant, silly mascot, a witness to every laugh, every inside joke. I'd send her poems, genuine and heartfelt lines spilling love onto the page, only to pivot abruptly into twisted humor that left her crying from laughter She called me a sick fuck with a grin that could disarm a priest.

And yeah, maybe I was. But her mouth? That wasn't the mouth of some angel sent to purify my soul. No—hers was more reminiscent of Deadpool's. Sharp. Relentless. Inappropriate at all the right times. And I loved that about her.

But while we both have a mouth that would make the devil blush, we could express our love freely with words. Once facing the daunting reality of our long-distance relationship, she asked me seriously, "How are we going to make this work?"

My response was simple: "One day at a time."

When she replied with uncertainty, I added, "The strongest steel has to be forged in the hottest fires—but once it's built, it's nearly indestructible."

She was filled with stunned laughter and had disbelief swirling behind her eyes, finally hit me with, "Who the hell are you?"

It was moments like those—beautifully absurd yet profoundly real—that defined us.

At Red Rocks, we stood beneath stars blinking like distant galaxies, the music from Illenium booming off ancient stone, echoing into the sky. I felt small, but not alone. That night was magic—the kind of moment that pulls wonder out of your bones. The next night, we found ourselves tucked into a tiny mountain venue outside Denver. No reception. Less than 200 people. Just rhythm, heat, and firelight flickering across faces. Illenium again—this time stripped down, raw. Intimate.

Later, in Pensacola, it was just us. A bottle of champagne. Cigars. Toes in the sand. The waves soft, the breeze warm. No music but the ocean. I looked up at the moon, full and glowing. Beautiful didn't cover it. In my head, I heard Travis's voice from a night just like this—soft, reverent: "The moon's beautiful tonight." And he was right. So was she.

Our lives were woven through these moments—the loud and quiet, the euphoric and calm. We balanced joy with grief. Melissa carried loss too—her cousin Dani, whom she spoke of with love that never faded, like starlight reaching across space long after the star itself had dimmed. I knew that grief intimately. Together, we allowed it space, neither running nor forcing it away.

Then came a different grief.

My grandma's health faltered. The woman who'd anchored my chaotic life lay fragile, hooked to machines. Melissa stood next to me as I broke—silent, steady, her hand warm in mine. We were called in to say goodbye.

But grandma didn't go that night. She walked out without the machines, her breath her own again. A quiet miracle that felt like a nod from the universe: Not yet.

With life reminding us how fleeting it could be, I decided to anchor something permanent. On a bench dedicated to Dani, beneath the endless sky, I proposed with a ring I'd earned outright. No debts, no doubts—just intent and sacrifice.

Life surged forward again, an opportunity arose—more stability, better future. Just as I was weighing the offer, Melissa handed me a wrapped box.

Inside?

A revelation that shifted our entire universe.

24

The Gentlemen

We were already flying—new life, new love, a fresh chapter unfolding in Chicago. I had finally found my footing again—momentum building, purpose clear, balance settling around me like a familiar coat. But the evening I stepped through our front door, tired and worn from a relentless day at work, I had no idea I was about to step into something far greater.

Melissa met me on the couch, her eyes glowing softly, a gift bag waiting patiently in her lap. No dramatic speech, no elaborate setup—just that quiet, knowing smile. Curiously, I reached inside, pushing past the soft rustle of tissue paper until my fingers brushed a small box. Inside, tucked neatly, sat a pair of tiny, all-white baby Converse—matching the pairs Melissa and I already owned.

My brain was still trapped between deadlines and meetings; the meaning didn't register immediately. But when it did, it hit me like an earthquake—laughter burst from me, joy tumbling out recklessly, followed swiftly by tears. I wrapped her tightly, holding onto her as if the world itself might spin away beneath us.

We were going to have a baby. All the pain, every devastating chapter, the wreckage we'd somehow managed to crawl out from under—it had brought us right here. New life. Our life. Together.

I already had two incredible kids—Kaden and Jersie—and I loved them fiercely. But this felt entirely different. This was about bringing a child into a home built on peace, laughter, and genuine love. Not the kind we'd had to fight for like air, nor the kind we had once bargained for with apologies but love that thrived without conditions or fear.

We hadn't been trying—no charts, calendars, or clinical timelines. Just an open-hearted "if it happens, it happens." And now it was undeniably happening.

I joked, "I bet we're having twins."

Melissa gave me that wide-eyed, incredulous look of hers—the one that said you're out of your mind. But there was history: her grandpa, aunts, cousins—twins ran deep in her family. Instinct stirred in my gut. We took eight tests, each one reinforcing the incredible truth.

Weeks later, we sat anxiously in the ultrasound room—Melissa lying on the table, a slick sheen of gel on her stomach, the tech scanning. I watched the screen intently, breath held, waiting for that tiny flicker of life.

I didn't see one.

I saw two.

"Oh," I whispered softly.

Melissa whipped her head toward me, worry flashing in her eyes. "What? What is it?"

The tech smiled knowingly, nodding toward me. "He already knows. There are two heartbeats."

Melissa gasped, eyes wide in shock and joy. "Oh my God!"

A triumphant smile spread across my face. "Told you."

Identical twins. Identical miracles.

We named them immediately—Baby A and Baby B. Baby B was restless, bouncing energetically around the screen, clearly eager to embrace life. Baby A was quieter, gentle and reserved, almost shy. We laughed, joking Baby B was clearly mine—loud, always moving—and Baby A was hers—thoughtful, calm, observant.

Melissa was sick constantly. Not just morning sickness— relentless waves hitting her at every hour. Her sense of smell became superhero-level sensitive; my freshly washed socks sent her running for fresh air. She didn't complain, though—she adapted gracefully, adjusting her diet and drinking filtered water. She did everything right.

We were flying high. Grateful. Nervous. Beautifully happy.

Then came the silence.

During one of our routine checkups, the tech's easy conversation fell into quiet concentration. Her brow furrowed, tension building in the room. Melissa and I locked eyes, a silent exchange of panic.

"I'm sorry," the tech said quietly, voice gentle. "I'm getting different NT measurements."

We didn't know what "NT" meant. She explained quickly—fluid measurements at the back of their necks, markers for chromosomal abnormalities. Baby B's measurement was off.

"Could indicate Down Syndrome," she murmured.

My heart plunged—not from rejection, but from fear. Fear of a harsher world, fear of complications, of their pain, their suffering. Melissa wept quietly. I pulled her close, holding her, promising her it would be okay, because hope was the only thing left to give.

We left silently, fear pooling heavy in our hearts. I buried the dread deep, refusing to speak it into existence. We saw specialists, another ultrasound.

Relief. Measurements returned within range. Maybe we'd escaped disaster.

Then came the genetic counselor, her tone soft, her words sharp as glass, cutting through our newfound calm with phrases like "selective termination." My world froze. We had just seen our babies—alive, vibrant, our boys—and now someone was suggesting choosing between them?

The doctor followed with more worry: uneven growth. Possible Twin Twin Transfusion Syndrome—one baby receiving too much blood, the other too little. Words like needles, high risk, loss. Not yet, he said, not today, but monitor closely.
Week after week we watched our boys—Jackson, vibrant and lively, Grayson, gentle and steadfast. Our little gentlemen. Each scan, I fell harder. Imagining their laughter, their first steps, their childhood adventures.

Then came the day—the full scan meant to take hours. The tech began, stopping abruptly. Concern creased her forehead deeply. She fetched the doctor, urgency thick in the air.

Melissa's hand tightened desperately around mine.

"She's dilated," the doctor said. "Nineteen weeks. It's too soon."

Words shattered around us like fragile glass. We cried, clinging to each other, fear clawing at our throats. They suggested a cerclage—stitching her cervix closed. But they had to wait twenty-four terrifying hours, watching for infection.

That night, we lay in a sterile hospital bed, shadows deep and dark around us, air sharp with antiseptic and uncertainty. My hand rested on Melissa's belly, whispering pleas to Jackson and Grayson, begging them to hold tight, to stay just a bit longer.

Morning came painfully slow. A portable ultrasound machine was quietly wheeled in—one final look before surgery.

There they were—Jackson, ever-moving, and Grayson, quietly strong. Alive. Beautiful.

It might be the last glimpse I'd ever have.

I cupped Melissa's face gently, kissed her forehead deeply, whispered I loved her, and watched helplessly as they rolled her away, praying to any god or force that might hear me, pleading desperately into the silent universe:

"Please. Let them stay."

In that moment, every star I'd ever wished upon seemed heartbreakingly silent.

25

Jackson & Grayson

I walked the halls of the hospital like a ghost—no direction, no destination. Each step felt disembodied, like someone else was steering my body through the sterile corridors. The fluorescent lights buzzed overhead, a droning hum that matched the numb static filling my chest.

Melissa had come out of surgery. The doctor was optimistic, confident even. He said everything had gone perfectly, a rare reassurance amid weeks of uncertainty. Melissa, groggy from anesthesia, drifted in and out of consciousness, but even then, her first whispered words were, "Are they okay?"

They wheeled the ultrasound machine back in, the screen flickering softly to life. Two tiny heartbeats appeared—quick, rhythmic pulses. And then Grayson, my quiet one, the shy one who seemed to hide from the world, turned and looked directly at us. It lasted only a second, but it was as if he knew we were watching. His tiny face stared out from the screen, long enough to reassure me, long enough to say, "I'm okay, Dad." Then he turned away, back into the safety of his brother's shadow.

I let out the breath I didn't realize I'd been holding.

The doctor entered again, reiterating his optimism. He seemed genuinely hopeful. For a brief moment, I allowed myself to believe we had finally turned a corner. Then came that fucking word again:

"However."

He was still concerned. The Twin Twin Transfusion Syndrome wasn't getting better—it was getting worse. Jackson was growing rapidly, kicking and spinning, always vibrant, always moving. Grayson remained gentle, patient, calm—but falling further behind.

I threw myself into research, poring over medical journals, clinical studies, forum posts filled with statistics and outcomes. I convinced myself that knowing everything was some kind of armor. That if I understood it deeply enough, I could somehow shield us from what was coming.

But no amount of reading prepares you for the reality of loss.

We were referred to a specialist for laser ablation surgery—a terrifying procedure that would sever the shared blood vessels between the twins. It might save them. Or we could lose one, possibly both. The options felt cruel, impossible. We scheduled it anyway, holding tightly to any shred of hope.

That night, Melissa mentioned feeling pressure, discomfort like a UTI. She called the doctor, who calmly suggested we come in—"just to be safe."

We drove forty-five minutes in tense silence, the hospital looming like a fortress. When the doctor examined Melissa, the room turned cold.

Her voice faltered, eyes heavy with the truth she was about to deliver. "You're dilated to seven centimeters."

Melissa's scream ripped through me like shrapnel. "Fuck!" She cried—a sound so raw, so guttural, that I fell apart along with her.

We sobbed openly, desperately. There was no filter, no dignity—just sheer, brutal grief. It felt primal, unrecognizable, foreign yet deeply familiar. Guilt surged through me, ruthless and punishing. Guilt for having hope. Guilt for believing we might escape the worst.

Then came another choice—deliver our sons or let them slip away unseen. We couldn't let them go silently. They were real, they had names, faces, personalities already. Jackson kicked Grayson on ultrasounds; Grayson had looked at me, just once, to say it was okay. They deserved to be held.

I called our mothers. Melissa's mom first, urgency and heartbreak cracking my voice. Then mine—her sobs echoed in my ears, deeper than I'd ever heard from her before.

And I had to say it aloud, the words sticking like glass shards in my throat:

"The boys are coming... but they won't stay."

Fear invaded next—not just grief. What would our sons look like? Would there be pain? Would their tiny bodies feel suffering? Would I regret seeing them? Would they seem too small... too fragile... would it be too hard to love?

I bent down to Melissa's belly, pressing my forehead to her skin, whispering words I hoped could reach them. "I love you both. Jackson, take care of your brother. Stay close to each other."

When they administered the epidural, Melissa cried harder—not from pain, but from the loss of their movement. It was her last physical connection to them, the last proof they were still there, alive inside her. Gone in an instant.

I panicked silently, haunted by thoughts I couldn't voice: Are they scared? Do they know what's happening?

I stepped out to breathe, just for a moment. When I returned, a nurse asked gently, "Do you want to be in here?" In my confusion, I stepped back out, only realizing seconds later what she meant. I rushed back, gripping Melissa's hand tightly, whispering over and over how much I loved her.

At 7:11 a.m., Grayson Gregory Borchers was born—twelve ounces of delicate perfection. My heart stuttered. I couldn't look, not yet.

At 7:19 a.m., Jackson Finn Borchers joined his brother, weighing just over a pound, already fiercely protective, even in this moment.

I finally forced myself to look. And what I saw wasn't terrifying or grotesque—it was pure, heartbreaking beauty. My sons were tiny, fragile, perfectly formed. They were breathtaking.

Melissa and I cradled them, their faint heartbeats fluttering softly. Jackson and Grayson, our little gentlemen. We whispered every promise, every hope, every dream we had for them. We told them how deeply loved they were, how desperately wanted.

And when their heartbeats faded into silence, we still held them, refusing to let go. Not yet. Not ever fully.
In that room, surrounded by broken dreams and unbearable silence, we found a fierce love in our boys—a love that would never diminish, never fade, even in the brutal shadow of grief.

Because Jackson and Grayson were ours. Our sons. And we would carry them forever.

26

We stayed with them as long as we could, holding onto those fleeting, sacred moments as if they might somehow stretch into forever. But when the time finally came, we faced a decision no parent ever imagines. We chose cremation—not because it felt easy, but because it meant our boys would never be far from us. Wherever life took us, they would be right there, carried close.

Their ashes rest in a sky-blue, heart-shaped urn, etched with words we chose carefully the only words that ever felt right:

Our Gentlemen.

That weekend was meant to be filled with final touches for the baby shower. Instead, we found ourselves numb and hollow in a cold, sterile funeral home, making arrangements for two perfect little boys who never got the chance to open their eyes.

As grief settled deep into our bones, the world around us continued turning, indifferent and cruel.

Melissa's workplace poured out love in waves of compassion. They held her close, gave her space to grieve openly, and let her fall apart without judgment. Her boss called me personally, his voice soft but firm, saying, "You take care of our girl. I'm sending all my love."

My workplace? My friends? Their response was different—an emptiness that echoed louder than any words could.

Work was a cold monotone. A shallow, empty, "Sorry to hear that," followed by deafening silence.

I reached out to Mark. No answer. I texted him, told him about Jackson and Grayson, about our devastating loss. His reply came quickly enough—he said he was crying, promised he'd call.

I waited a day. A week. A month. Silence.

I called again. Nothing. Eventually, quietly, I deleted his number. I tried Kiley next. No answer, just a text: "Hey, busy. What's up?"

"I just really need to talk," I replied, vulnerability seeping through every letter.

She responded bluntly, "I'm with my boyfriend, can't right now."

I tried again, softer, pleading: "If you get a minute, I could really use a friend."

She fired back: "I'll be busy the next couple days."

"One minute," I begged. "Just someone to talk to."

"You're being too needy." Her words were sharp, cruel, dismissive.

Me—the one who'd sat for hours listening, guiding her through meltdowns, relationships, and career crossroads. I hadn't asked for advice, just presence, just a human voice in the darkness. Even that was too much.

She never even asked why. Never asked about the boys.

I told her to take every reference she ever got from me and shove it up her ass.

Because in the worst moment of my life, I learned who was truly in my corner.

And it wasn't the people I'd spent years supporting.

From my boss, a single, indifferent sentence. Not a card. Not a call. And when I explained I wasn't ready to return yet, he asked coldly:

"When do you think you'll be back?"

I snapped, my voice shaking with restrained fury, "You tell me how long it takes to bury your sons, and I'll give you a fucking date."

He stumbled over his words, awkwardly walking it back. "Take the whole month, if you need it."

A month—as if grief had an expiration date, a tidy end point.

I asked for help filing Short-Term Disability. Silence. Asked again. Still nothing.

Meanwhile, coworkers kept texting about spreadsheets, metrics, reports—cold data points in a moment when my entire world was ashes.

Eventually, desperate, I went above him, pleading with his boss to intervene, just to get the calls to stop. She hadn't even been informed of what had happened.

By the time I returned, the damage was irreversible. I walked back into chaos—short-staffed, exhausted, abandoned. I'd asked my boss to help interview candidates. He didn't. I'd asked him to support my assistants.

"I sent an email," he said flatly.

An email.

Then he insisted on a meeting—with my assistants, to discuss "communication." No "How are you?" No "What do you need?" Just performance metrics. In that moment, something broke inside me, something profound and permanent:

Men aren't allowed to grieve.

Not openly. Not in corporate America. Not if you're the one who's supposed to be strong.

Days later, he walked in with another district manager I'd never met. They closed the door, launching into a ninety-minute interrogation, their voices harsh enough for customers to overhear.

The stranger's opening line?

"What's your problem? Why do you have such a chip on your shoulder?"

No humanity. No empathy. Just corporate poison wrapped in a suit and tie.

I shut down completely, silent and numb. It was the only way to survive their words.

At the end, as an afterthought, they muttered, "Sorry for your loss," as if checking a box.

All I could think was: My sons are dead. My fiancé is wrecked. I'm barely breathing. And you're worried about fucking KPIs.

My nervous system shut down and I went numb.

But my team? They saw me. They knew. They named a star after Jackson and Grayson, handing me a certificate that felt like oxygen in a room where I'd forgotten how to breathe. For someone who always found meaning in the night sky, it meant everything.

Melissa and I took a trip to Sioux City to see the kids and Grandma. Melissa hadn't seen Grandma since that terrifying hospital stay, the one with tubes and whispered prayers. When we walked in, Grandma cracked a joke immediately. Melissa laughed—a sound I hadn't heard in weeks. That's how they met, not in sorrow, but in laughter.

Grandma opened up to us in a way she never had. She spoke candidly about losing Chad, about chasing desperate treatments, even risking arrest to save her son. She confessed to the soul-deep grief she carried when Jeff died, about contemplating suicide, the anger she held toward God. There was no polished, scripted comfort—just raw, human honesty.

Melissa saw her clearly for the first time—not just as my grandma, but as the woman who shaped me, who loved me, who anchored me.

Now Melissa understood why I never just called her grandma.

She was Mom.

But even with that connection, I still felt invisible elsewhere. Friends I'd known for years vanished. Family scattered, distant. Melissa had her circle, her comfort. But me? I felt forgotten, transparent.

People offered condolences, always focused on Melissa:

"So sorry for Melissa's loss...oh, and Dan's too." An afterthought, every time.

I wrote a eulogy online, a desperate attempt to make the world see Jackson and Grayson, to acknowledge their brief, beautiful existence. Hundreds replied, pouring love and support.

For Melissa.

When they mentioned me, I was an addendum: "Praying for Melissa...and Dan."

Grief curled inward, hardened into anger. Melissa begged me to open up, to share.

But how could I? She was barely holding together. One of us had to stand firm.

I swallowed it down, internalized the rage and helplessness.

I thought work would anchor me. It didn't. Every day I carried two names no one wanted to say:

Jackson. Grayson.

Amid that aching silence, we did something important. At Cook County courthouse, we got married—not for show, but for them, for us, to honor our boys.

Melissa's mom and Brian stood by us. Brian quietly recorded our vows, our quiet promises whispered in a sterile government room.

No fanfare. Just truth. Just love.

We spent the evening with Brian, holding teddy bears meant for our sons, and Brian wept with us.

Because real friends show up—not just for the joy, but for the grief.

And they stay, holding onto love, even when it hurts.

27

My Brother

March 30, 2019.

Three days after the boys were born and died, I got a text from Travis:

Hey bro, I am deeply sorry for your family. I couldn't think of anything worse an individual could go through. If you need anything at all or just want to talk I'm here for you. I hope Kaden and Jersie are doing okay. I can't fathom what Melissa must be going through having to carry them boys. Give her a hug. Be her rock. You two take all the time you need to find peace, brother. There's no book on how to deal with this sort of thing—just love each other the best you can and know tomorrow will be better than today.

My reply came from somewhere between devastation and gratitude:

Thank you, brother. That means more than you know. I appreciate your support and love. Kaden and Jersie are hurt, but they're healing. I'm holding strong for Melissa—I'm not going to let this define or crush us. This is the most excruciating pain I've ever experienced. You were there when my grandpa passed, and you know how much that hurt. But this? This is a whole different level. I know I'll learn to live with the pain in time. Right now… we're just angry and hurt. Thank you, man.

Less than two weeks later, Travis's life changed forever.

A man broke into his home.

There was a struggle. A fight. A gunshot.

When the dust settled, Travis was standing over the body of the intruder.

I reached out immediately, fingers shaking as I typed, heart pounding in my ears:
Hey man. I just heard the news. First of all, I'm glad you and your daughter are safe. Second, I can't imagine the emotions you're going through, but I'm thankful you're alive. I'm sorry you had to live through this and just know I'm here for you—just like you said you'd be here for me.

His reply was short. Heavy:

Thanks Dan. Crazy shit. Just glad Magdalena was with her mom.

I replied:

If you need anything, man—vent, cry, sit in silence—I'm here. Anytime.

Reading Travis's short reply, I imagined him standing there— gun smoke still sharp in the air, ears ringing, heart racing—and realized he'd survived something unimaginable. A silence settled in my chest, cold and heavy as stone. I meant every word I said to him. I knew—even in selfdefense—that kind of trauma cuts deep. It leaves wounds no one else can see. I prayed I'd never have to fully understand it.

The weeks moved forward. Because the world doesn't stop. But I did. I was frozen in time.

I walked through work like a ghost. Returning after losing your children felt like showing up to class after being abducted by aliens—everyone awkwardly staring, half-expecting you to share something profound, half-terrified you actually would. My boss? Absent. The grief that had once been cautiously acknowledged was now something that made people look away.

I lost my voice.

So, I went quiet. Cynical. Detached. Everything started feeling distant, like I was watching my life from behind soundproof glass. Anger became my language. I hyper-fixated on injustice—on systems that failed people, on corporate greed, on fake leaders who talked empathy but never showed it. The more I tried to find meaning, the more everything unraveled. I wasn't building anything anymore—I was just surviving.

And no one really asked how I was doing. They asked about Melissa.

I was still trying to be a husband. Still trying to be a dad to two kids with grief-soaked hearts.
Still trying to remember who I used to be.
But while I was falling apart, the world kept spinning. Faster. Louder. More demanding.

I spiraled at work. But in the background—someone kept showing up.

Brian.

One of the guys I met through Instagram. At first, just another meme creator. But he started checking in. Regularly. Quietly.

You're not alone, man.
Love you, brother.
You're still moving forward.

Jokes. Memes. Quotes. Random dumb shit that somehow landed exactly when I needed it to. And it mattered.

We started texting every day. Built something real. No drama. No expectations. Just steady presence.

He helped us move. He became family. For the first time since Travis, I felt like someone truly saw me. Like I wasn't invisible.

That friendship—and a message on LinkedIn—pulled me out of the wreckage.

It was a new job opportunity. Lower pay. But it came with something far more valuable: a chance to rebuild.

I took a lateral position at another company. Smaller team, same title, same responsibilities. A clean slate. A moment to slow down and catch my breath.

At least, that was the idea.

But I came in too hot. Burned by grief. Covered in the ash of everything I'd just lived through. My leadership was mechanical. Cold. HR got involved. My empathy was buried beneath exhaustion and unprocessed rage. I wasn't building culture—I was checking boxes.

Then, in the middle of all that noise…

Melissa got pregnant again.
We were cautious. Hopeful. Guarded.

But something felt different.

The company offered three months of paid paternity leave—
even to fathers. No laptop. No emails. No expectations. Just
time.

We needed it.

We found out we were having a girl. We named her London
Yvonne—Yvonne for her grandmother. Her name felt like a
poem. A promise. A breath after the longest exhale.

London was born March 20, 2020. Holding her, tiny body warm,
scent impossibly sweet, tears came instantly. I pressed my cheek
gently against her soft, reddish hair, memorizing her first tiny
cries. Grief and joy collided inside me, leaving me shaking with
relief and sorrow for the brothers she'd never meet.

COVID hit. Masks, sanitizer, anxiety around every corner. Yet
hidden within was intimacy— Melissa sleeping beside me,
London's tiny breaths syncing with mine. We were protecting
something sacred.

The world reopened slowly. My return to work synced with the
world blinking back to life. Time had paused with me—and now
moved again.

Family fractured, splintered by something death hadn't managed
to break. COVID wedged invisible walls—politics, vaccines.
Calls dwindled, invites stopped. Message received. Our circle
tightened. Then came July.

Jersie's birthday was coming up, and nearly a year had passed since I'd seen the kids in person. So, I loaded up and drove back to Sioux City.

We stayed at my great-grandpa's house. My mom lived there now, having returned after her divorce to help care for Grandma. The house was quiet—familiar and sacred all at once. Sitting within its walls felt comforting yet surreal, especially when Jersie began sharing a story about selling fundraiser chocolate bars and running into Travis. Of course, he'd bought one. She said he asked about me, reminisced, smiled as he spoke.

Then Josh—my youngest brother—stopped by.

Josh had seen Travis too. They talked for a bit, caught up, mostly about me. Josh held my gaze for a moment, sincerity clear in his eyes.

"I think that dude misses you, man," he said gently. "You should give him a call."
I nodded, promising him—and myself—that I would. I'd just gotten back to Chicago and needed rest first. Sunday slipped by quietly. I figured Monday would be soon enough. After all, I thought we still had time.

Monday morning arrived slow and heavy, exhaustion from the travel still clinging to my bones. Sunlight seeped in reluctantly. The dull glow sharpened into an unwelcome wakefulness. My limbs felt anchored to the bed, muscles stiff, body drained. I blinked away the grogginess, fighting to rise through layers of sleep that refused to release me.

Then my phone rang—sharp, insistent, cutting straight through the haze.

My chest tightened immediately. Something felt off, dread pooling in the pit of my stomach. The screen flashed Ashleigh's name.

She rarely called when a text always works and would never call this early.

I answered, bracing myself, heart suddenly racing like I'd been startled awake from a nightmare.

She was sobbing, broken, gasping between breaths.

"Dan…"

Her voice cracked. My throat closed.

"Don't say it," I whispered, desperate, my heartbeat roaring in my ears, the room spinning slightly around me.

"Dan, I have to tell you…"

My fingers went numb, every nerve on edge, as if my body already knew what my mind refused to accept.

"Don't say it," I begged quietly. "Who was it?"

Silence stretched, deep enough to drown in. Then, barely audible through her tears, her voice broke through:

"…Dan… Travis committed suicide."

The words detonated inside my chest, shattering everything. A sudden, icy numbness surged through me. My vision blurred, ears ringing with a deafening silence that swallowed the room. The phone nearly slipped from my trembling fingers as reality tilted, fractured, and collapsed beneath me.

Not Travis.

28

Fission

There are chapters you dread writing and this is another one. Not because they're hard—but because they hurt.

This is one of them.

And I don't even know if "hurt" is the right word. It doesn't feel like a wound. It feels like a severing. Like someone took the one last thread tethering me to some version of wholeness and cut it in silence, then walked away.

Travis was my brother.

Not by blood. Not by paperwork. Not by shared childhood streets or family trees. He was my always. My anchor. As long as he was breathing somewhere in the world, I could keep going. No matter how bad it got—Travis was the North Star I never questioned.

And then, just like that, he was gone.

And I was unmoored. No gravity. No compass. Just drift. Just dark.

I didn't just cry. I wept. I shook. I collapsed. Not just from losing him but because his death tore open every sealed vault, I thought I'd welded shut. Every loss. Every betrayal. Every buried ache I thought I could outwork, outrun, or out lift came rushing in like a tidal wave of ghosts.

It hit like a fucking bomb.
The atom was once thought to be the smallest thing that
mattered. Tight. Elegant. Contained. A nucleus of protons and
neutrons, hugged by electrons in perfect orbit—a balance so
delicate, it holds up the known world.

But rupture that core— split it open— and the energy released is
catastrophic.

A single atom, unzipped, becomes fire. Becomes fallout.
Becomes death in the air, in the soil, in the marrow of anything
still trying to live.

They call it fission.

I call it grief.

Because when death cracked the nucleus of my life—when
Travis, when my twins, when dreams I hadn't even dared to
name were suddenly gone—everything I knew was vaporized.
First came the blinding flash—the moment I knew. Then the
silence. The disbelief. The scream of everything that would
never be again.

And then the fallout.

The long, choking half-life of loneliness.
The dust in my lungs every time I try to say his name.
The radiation of memory becoming silent, invisible, deadly.

Science says destruction isn't the end. That matter reforms. That
energy moves.

But the universe never forgets the split.

And neither do I.

That day, when I found out, something unhooked inside me.
Melissa remembers the sound of my voice cracking when I got
the news from Ashleigh. She said her heart broke just hearing
mine collapse. But she didn't even know the full weight of what
was behind her broken husband. The layers that slammed down
all at once. The pieces I was already trying to carry.

Because Travis wasn't just my friend.

He was the one I ran to. My protector. My mirror. My steady.
And I should've been that for him. I should've called. I
should've fucking called.

I know it might not have changed anything. But Jesus Christ—I
would've told him, I see you. I hear you. I'm with you. I
would've reminded him who the fuck he was.

But I didn't. And now I'll never know.

The grief came in waves. Relentless. No air in between. I was
drowning in it, and the one person who always threw me a
rope... was gone.

Melissa tried. God bless her, she tried. But this wasn't one loss.
This wasn't a moment. This was a reckoning. This was the
death of everything I had held sacred—

Loved ones. Purpose. Friendship. Loyalty. Myself.

And she didn't realize—when she tried to help me grieve Travis—that I was also carrying the ashes of so many other losses. That I'd been boiling in silence for years.

That first COVID summer, I got in my car and drove to Iowa. Back to say goodbye. Melissa stayed home with baby London. I made that seven-and-a-half-hour drive solo, heart heavy, silence louder than any playlist.

Somewhere near Waterloo, my phone rang.

It was my mom.

"Have you heard from Josh?" she asked, casually.

I said no.

She hesitated. "I was just wondering how he's doing…"

That fucking stabbed me.

I was in the middle of a grief-soaked highway, en route to a memorial for the brother I just lost— and she's asking about Josh?

"Josh still has fucking Nate!" I snapped, nearly yelling into the phone.

Do you know what it feels like to have your heart broken while you're already heartbroken? To be in free fall and still have someone ask if another person's okay—as if you're not the one bleeding?

When I got to the memorial, I hugged his mom. Hugged his aunt. Saw faces from another lifetime. My mom and Josh sat with me. Ashleigh was there, her boyfriend Eric. Jamie. A few others. People who knew the version of me that only Travis could bring out.

We told stories. Taco Bell runs. Pool hall nights. The way he'd twist a joke and leave you doubled over, or how he'd debate you into the ground and still make you feel like you won.

We laughed. We cried. And it helped. It didn't fix anything—but it helped.

But grief doesn't care if you're still healing. It doesn't pause the calendar.

I had to return to Illinois. We were packing to move closer to my new store—another fresh start, whatever the hell that means.

I'd only been there six months. My boss? Four. But unlike the last place, where no one could comprehend what it meant to bury your sons... this time, they understood. They didn't rush me. They showed grace. And I didn't realize until then how deeply I needed it.

We moved. Packed up what little still felt like home. Transferred everything to Algonquin.

Brian showed up, like he always did. Helped us move. Lifted boxes while we talked—about Travis, about memories, about the fucked-up beauty of life. It was therapy. It helped.

But even Brian didn't know the truth.

No one did.

Because something had already started growing inside me. Something quiet. Dark.

That seed of guilt I had buried? It had begun to sprout. And what it was growing into was hatred.

Not toward anyone else.

Toward me.

I couldn't attend the funeral. Due to Covid restrictions and work precautions, my kind of luck. I wrote a letter for my mom to read it aloud at the service.

"There really aren't enough words in the world to describe Travis. I always have and always will say Travis was nobody's friend because he was everyone's best friend.
I don't remember high school without him. He's always been my little big brother. He looked out for me, and I looked out for him—no matter who was in the wrong.
From pool halls to basketball courts to lazy afternoons swimming, he made every day better. He made every day the best day.

I remember when he called me after his Iowa Standardized Test results. He asked me to pick him up for lunch. When I got there, he was beaming. Said he scored number one in the state. Was gonna meet the mayor and everything. And for a year straight, every argument ended with him saying, 'Dan, I would know. I was number one in the whole state.'

That was Travis. Brilliant. Hilarious. Loving. He could debate you into a corner and still leave you laughing.

But more than that, he loved. Deeply. Quietly. Steadily.
I wish I could be there today. I really do. But I want everyone to
know:

You've always been—and will always be—my guardian.
You've always been—and will always be—my brother.
I love you. I miss you. Every single fucking day."

But the letter didn't bring me closure.

Because closure is a myth.

And that seed of self-hatred?

It wasn't just sprouting.

It started blooming.

29
The Hours Between

There was no warning. No shift in the air. Just another night like any other—until it wasn't. Until it turned into something else entirely.

I was with him. Travis.

We were surrounded by family—though I couldn't tell you who. The details blurred like smudged paint. Unimportant. He was the only thing I could focus on. His presence anchored everything.

He told me he was leaving.

That's when it hit me—he was already gone. I felt it in my chest, like something tearing loose from the inside. A snap of reality. I knew where he was going. I knew what he was about to do. And for the first time since losing him, it felt like maybe—just maybe—I had a chance to stop it.

I turned to follow.

But before I could, he locked me in a room. A heavy click. A steel door between us.

I pounded against it, fists raw, voice cracked and shaking. "Please, Trav! Let me out!"

His voice came through the door. Calm. Steady. Heavy. "You can't stop me, Dan."

"I know," I said, desperation curling in my throat. "I know I can't. Just let me out."

Silence.

Then he asked, almost curious, almost sad: "Then why do you want out?"

The lock clicked and I stepped into the hallway and there he was—standing still, waiting for me. His face... God, his face. It was pain, but not the kind you wear. It was laced through every line. Pain that hurt just to look at.

"So I can have one day with you," I whispered. "Just one day, man. I won't try to fix anything. I won't justify life. I just want a day."

He looked at me like he didn't believe it. Like he was trying to see if I was lying—to him or to myself.

But he nodded.

And the world shifted.

Now there were more people. His family. Mine. Ashleigh. Faces I half-remembered, half-felt. I told them all Travis was already gone. That this was a miracle, something borrowed, something unreal. No one believed me. They pointed to him—smiling, laughing, alive.

"See? He's fine," they said.

But he looked at me from across the room, and I saw it in his eyes. He knew.

So I shifted the moment.

"Let's make it a Travis Day," I said. "Let's cook his favorite food, bring him his favorite drinks and desserts. Let's celebrate him—for everything he's ever been to us."

Everyone agreed. They got to work, bustling through the dream like it was a party.

Travis shrugged and wandered into another room.

I got distracted—helping, laughing, moving through rooms like memories. Until suddenly, I realized… I didn't know where he was.

I searched, room to room, and found him sitting quietly.

He was holding a baby.

Tickling them. Trying to make them laugh. It wasn't London.

It was a boy.

I think it was Jackson. Or Grayson.
And I heard another baby cry from somewhere else. A twin cry. Same rhythm. Same ache.

He looked up and met my eyes.
"I'm still here," he said. "I didn't go anywhere."
Then the moment jumped again.

The party was nearly ready. More people arrived. Hundreds now. The dream thickened like a memory too sacred to forget. Travis was asleep on the couch, his head shaved except for a bleached rat tail—because of course it was. That was Travis. Always trying to make us laugh even when we didn't want to.

I bent down and whispered, "Hey bro, you can sleep in my bed if you want. No need to crash on the couch."

He grinned. "Like the good ol' days, right? I remember that. You'd sleep on the floor."

I laughed. "Yeah... I probably will again."

Then time jumped again.

The house was full. The music low. The food warm. I made us drinks and handed one to Ashleigh. "I'll go get Trav," I said.

He was just stepping out of the shower.

"Hey man," I said, trying to keep it light. "Everyone's ready. It's all almost done."

He looked at me, tired. Agitated.
"What are you doing, Dan? What's this all for?"

I swallowed the lump in my throat.

"Because I want you to see it. All the love in this world for you." His eyes dropped. A shadow passed over his face. "It won't change anything. You know that, right?"

I broke.

Tears filled my eyes as I said, "Trav, you're not here. I know that. I know you're gone. But you're standing in front of me and I can't pretend it doesn't matter. I want to stop it. I want to change it. I'm in so much fucking pain, man. I'm hurting so bad…"

He cut me off.

"Welcome to my hell."

And I opened my eyes.

3:33 a.m, July 21, 2020. I cried and opened my notes on my iPhone and typed every detail and laid in bed until the kids woke up around 6:00 a.m. I wondered if I'd see him again or not.

Six days later, he came back.

This time, it was just us. Sitting together in a park. Quiet. No chaos. No background noise.

Just peace.

We were laughing. Quoting Stewie Griffin in those stupid exaggerated voices. Over-pronouncing silent Hs—"hwhip," "hwhat," "hwho." It felt easy. It felt like home.

I looked at him. Really looked.

"Trav, I want you to know I love you, man. I'm sorry I haven't always been there like you were for me."

He rolled his eyes. "Don't make this all weird."

Then he laughed. "But I love you too."

His smile—God, it lit up everything.

Then I noticed his outfit.

A cop uniform.

"Bro… why the hell are you dressed like a cop?"

He smirked. "Dan, it's your dream. You tell me."

I laughed. "Wait… what dream?"

I looked down at my hands. Tried to ground myself.

When I looked back up, he was gone.

But I heard his voice. Not loud. Not clear. More like a wind.
Like something brushing against my soul:

"I'm sorry, man. I'm really sorry. It wasn't supposed to be like
this. It was an accident."

I opened my eyes.

3:31 a.m, July 27, 2020. I opened my notes again with tears
rolling down my face and typed everything I could remember as
fast as I could. And for years, those dreams sat in my notes,
known only to Melissa and Ashleigh.

I don't know what those dreams meant.

But I felt them and here's something I can't shake:

My uncle, Lance Corporal Jeffrey Allan Borchers, was murdered while on duty in Hawaii. The exact time of death?

3:30 a.m.

A moment that cracked my family's foundation. A time I never forgot.

So what does it mean that these dreams came to me then? Right in that window—between 3:31 and 3:33 a.m.? That I was with Travis in the hours between?

I don't have the answers.

I'm not here to decode dreams or push some spiritual pitch.

But I felt them.

And if grief has a language, maybe this was part of it. A goodbye. A visit. A gift. Or maybe just the echo of love that refuses to stay dead.

Whatever it was… it was real to me.

And I won't forget it.

30

Leading While Bleeding

The world kept turning. Over it, that fiery bastard in the center of our solar system kept burning, dragging us along on some cosmic carousel, our little planet orbiting something bigger, which orbited something even bigger, all of it drifting through a vast and uncaring universe.

And yet, I was frozen.

Everything in the universe was in motion, but I was stuck. Paralyzed. Suspended in a moment I couldn't escape.

I went back to work.

Not because I wanted to. Not because I was ready. But because the world doesn't give a fuck about grief timelines. It demands that you clock in.

From the jump, something in me had shifted. I wasn't angry. I wasn't barking orders about KPIs or cracking jokes to hype the team. I wasn't loud or intense or driving performance through fire. I was quiet. Hollow. The light was gone.

And that silence—my absence of heat—scared the shit out of them.

They'd seen me at war with goals and pressure. They'd seen me lead through storm and fire. But they hadn't seen me like this. Stoic. Still. Not withdrawn, but not fully present either. Like a shadow of the guy, they used to follow.

One day, a customer got in my face about their bill—arms flying, voice rising, full dramatic rage mode. I stood there. Still. Calm. Didn't flinch. Didn't fire back. Not because I was controlling myself, but because I was empty. There was nothing left to react with. I had already lost more than a billing issue could threaten.

My team watched it all. One of my employees stepped in, de-escalated the whole thing, and then quietly told the customer I had just lost a close friend. That's when the customer came back. Put a hand on my shoulder. Looked me in the eye.

"I'm sorry for the way I acted. The world keeps moving. You'll be okay."

And something in me cracked. Not in a bad way. More like a thaw. A hairline fracture in the frozen stillness I'd been trapped in.

My team gave a damn—not just about my numbers, not just about what I produced—but about me.

It changed everything.

I started leading differently. I started listening harder. Watching posture. Noticing pauses. I didn't just ask, "What's your goal this month?" I asked, "Are you okay today?"

I stopped waiting for people to raise their hands and say, "I need help." Because I knew now— sometimes people can't ask. I couldn't. I didn't. It's one of the reasons why I'm writing this book in the first place. Because vulnerability isn't something you either have or don't. It's shaped by what you survive. What you're taught. What you're allowed to show.

Empathy became the lens.

Curiosity became the tool.

Not to drive numbers—but to understand people.

And ironically? It skyrocketed performance. Because people work harder when they feel seen.

Things started to stabilize. One day, my VP—someone I deeply respect—came through for a visit. We talked shop, talked future, talked impact. She pulled me aside and said, "You need to go to a bigger store. You've shown what you can do here. Now prove you can replicate it on a larger scale."

Within weeks, the opportunity opened. Bigger store. Bigger pressure. An hour away.

Melissa and I talked it out. I told her, "Short-term pain, long-term gain." Except my version of short-term was five years. But I had a plan. Always chess with me—never checkers.

So I took it.

Hour-long commute to Gurnee. Hour back to Algonquin. No shortcuts. No bullshit. Just a mission.

But I didn't walk into that store with a savior complex and a clipboard. I walked in like a human.

I sat with every single rep. One-on-one. Not to talk about goals. Not to review stats. Just to ask, "Who are you?"

And when they started to talk about work, I stopped them.

"Nope. I asked about you. Not the company. Not your title. You."

No HR small talk like "What's your favorite movie?" or "What motivates you?" I asked the real shit. I told them about growing up broke. About chasing money because I'd never had it. About losing Travis. About losing my sons. About grief.

I wasn't just their manager. I was a man. A husband. A father. A survivor.

And in that space, the walls came down. Trust went up.

We made changes.

They told me their feet hurt from standing on hard floors all day and I bought floor mats. Cushioned, supportive, real-deal mats. I didn't ask for permission, and I made it happen. Split the orders to spread the cost. When I told my director, I said, "Yeah, it was expensive. But now they're not in pain. And they can focus on customers instead of counting the minutes until they can sit down."

His reply, "Good call! Someone should have made that call sooner."

Breakroom too small? I cleared out the storage. Made space to breathe, to eat, and so they could just be human.

That's the job.

And with every step forward, I wasn't just leading I was also healing.

One day at a time.

Using everything grief had taught me. Everything Travis taught me. Everything Jackson and Grayson taught me.

Empathy. Curiosity. Depth.

That deep, soul-stirring need to make sure no one ever felt as lost as I had.

We blew the roof off that store.

Regional leaders started showing up. Word got around. I didn't care about the attention. I wasn't doing it for applause. I was doing it because I had purpose again. Fire again. And I wasn't done yet.

On May 29th, our son was born.

Kingston Daniel Borchers.

Our little dude shared a birthday with the friend I have had since 7th grade, Ashleigh. This little bald guy decided walking was a good idea at 8 months and 29 days. He was determined.

Stubborn. Hilarious. He waddled around like he'd been on his feet for years, chasing after London, trying to keep up.

We were celebrating life again.

And that's when death came calling. Again.

Grief doesn't wait for a standing ovation.

Beginning of December, I got the call.

Grandma was getting worse. Could be weeks. Could be days.

She was living in the house my great-grandfather built—the same house that held generations of love and pain. My mom was caring for her, doing everything she could.

And I knew.

I had to go.

I drove back to Sioux City. Walked into the house that raised me. Sat next to Grandma for eight hours. Just us. No distractions. No timeline. Just presence.

We talked about everything. My childhood. Her marriage. Chad. Jeff. Travis.

She lit up remembering Travis. Called him "Eddie Haskell"— that smart ass grin, that fake politeness that always masked a real heart.

Then, near the end, she got quiet. Her voice trembled. Her hands shook a little.

"I'm scared," she said. "What if I'm wrong? What if… there's nothing after this?"

I grabbed her hand. Looked her in the eyes.

"That's why it's called faith. Because you don't have to know. You just have to believe. And you do. You believe. So you're gonna see Jeff. Chad. Great grandpa. Travis. The boys. All of them.

And one day, I'll be there too—with all my stories. We'll be together again."

She kissed my forehead. I kissed hers.

"I love you, Graham-Graham."

"I love you, Danny."

That was the last time I saw her.

She passed on December 26th—the day after her favorite holiday.

She didn't go out kicking or clinging. She went out surrounded by memories. By grace. By the same spirit she poured into every cookie, every hug, every warm winter light.

And me?

I was tired.

Tired of losing moms.

Tired of losing pieces of myself.

I hadn't built a real community yet in Illinois. Just coworkers. Numbers. Performance targets. My circle felt smaller. Even Brian and I weren't texting as much.

Melissa was gutted. Grandma had helped her grieve after we lost the boys. They'd stayed up late talking about God, pain, and demons that would claw and naw at their thoughts. About what it means to keep going. For the first time, someone got it.

Grandma had lived a beautiful, hard, deeply intentional life.

And in the end?

No regrets. Just love. Just peace.

I accepted it. Not because it didn't hurt—but because it was her time.

Then, just when I thought maybe—just fucking maybe—I could start to breathe again…

My phone lit up.

Incoming call.

"Robert."

It was my dad.

31
Goodbye on the Wind

It had barely been thirty days since I buried my grandma.

My world was still cracked, still reeling, and I was doing my best to fake some version of normal. I was in the middle of interviewing for a promotion—a return to multi-unit leadership. Trying to prove I still had it. Trying to convince myself I still wanted it.

I had just finished the second interview when my phone rang.

It was him.

And in that moment, I knew—this call could only mean one of two things: someone we both knew was dying… or he was.

It had been ten fucking years since we last talked. Ten years since Grand Island. Ten years since I was still married to Ashley. Ten years of silence between us. Life had happened in the cracks. I had changed. I was different now—older, colder, sharper, and maybe, just maybe, more forgiving.

Maybe I could take the call.

Maybe we could be grown-ass men.

Maybe—after everything—I could try… one last fucking time.

I answered.

"Hello?"

His voice sounded weathered. Shaky. Like the words had to crawl over gravel just to reach air.

"Hey."

"Hey, Dan? It's Bob."

Awkward. Off to a great fucking start.

I sighed quietly. "Dad, I know it's you."

He grunted, like even hearing that acknowledgment rattled him. Then came the hammer.

"Oh… I thought you deleted my number. Or blocked it. Well… Dan… the cancer's back. But this time it's spread. I've got two tumors in my brain. It's not looking good."

There it was. The moment. The fucking bombshell.

He started detailing the situation like it was a medical lecture. One tumor operable, the other not. He talked about holding a cigarette and watching it fall from his hand without realizing it. Said he didn't even notice until it started burning his leg. His brain had already begun to betray him.

I drifted somewhere between shock and numbness. This was the man I had spent a lifetime trying to impress, trying to reach, trying to matter to. And now he was on a countdown.

"Turns out it's genetic," he added.

"Genetic?"

"Yeah... you need to start getting regular checkups, watch for the signs, avoid the triggers. Just... be aware."

All I could say was, "Damn."

We talked for another thirty minutes. He did most of the talking—filling me in on the last ten years like they were highlights on a sizzle reel. Concrete business, nice cars, camping trips, how he could smoke weed freely now. Bragging. Smirking. Living in a version of life where I'd never existed.

Then he asked how many kids I had. I told him. Gave him the run-down on Kaden, Jersie, London, Kingston, the boys. Mentioned Melissa.

Then he asked, "How's that buddy Travis of yours?"

My chest tightened like a vice.

Fuck you, I thought. It almost slipped out.

Instead, I forced the words: "He passed away. Year before last."

"Oh... sorry to hear that. Y'all were good friends, right?"

"Yep."

That was it.

We ended the call saying we'd stay in touch.

Shockingly, I got the promotion. By March, I was back in a multi-unit leadership role, firing on all cylinders. In Orlando, I was recognized as part of the top 3% of performers nationwide— three days of celebration, networking, and reflection.

I took Melissa to Mexico. We went to Cozumel, did the full thing—snorkeling, driving the island, tequila tastings, taco-stuffed days and saltwater-washed nights.

I started keto again. When I took the new role, I was pushing 300 pounds. The gym grind had vanished with the boys. I hadn't touched a weight since before they passed. So I started again. Quietly. Not for aesthetics. For control.

And I got to work.

Built curriculum. Developed leaders. Pushed results. I sprinted into every room like I was being hunted. I raised expectations. Raised standards. And my team? They rose with me.

In one of our check-ins, he gave me another update.

The news had worsened. One operation done. No fix. The timer was ticking down now.

I called my new boss who showed me he's a leader more than boss. My leader, Chidley, is a man I respect—stoic, sharp. Not overly emotional. But when I told him what was happening, his tone changed. Softened.

"This is just a job, Dan. You need to take care of your family. You need to take care of you."

He sounded like Travis.

And in that moment, I realized how rare grace really is. Real grace. Grace that doesn't ask for receipts or timelines.

I said it out loud for the first time: "My dad is dying."

The words landed like a stone in my chest. Heavy. Still.

I didn't run. But I pulled back. I started researching chemo and brain deterioration. I didn't want the end to be a fight—not for his sake. For mine. I didn't want to carry another ugly ending.

Then came the money talk.

He asked about my job. How much I made. Tried to sell me his truck. Asked me to buy his ticket to Illinois. Said he needed to meet his grandkids.

No. Absolutely fucking not.

Their first—and only—time meeting their grandpa wouldn't be like this. Wouldn't be him at the end. Wouldn't be dying eyes and trembling hands and medical devices. I'd already watched someone I love drift out of this world. I wasn't putting them through that again.

And this time, when I set the boundary… he didn't fight it.

He let it stand.

Then he sent me an email.

It was a mess. Rambling. Raw. A mix of apology and confession. He talked about gambling. Fights with his wife. Being treated like a child. He wrote about humiliation. About being voiceless in his own home. He said he was lost. That he loved me. That he hoped we could see each other before it got worse. And suddenly, so much made sense.

The missing money. The constant talk about it. The stress. The excuses. It clicked into place like a puzzle I didn't know I'd been trying to solve—he was a gambler. When he got out of prison, he didn't shake the addiction… he just swapped it. Replaced drugs with dice. Needles with numbers. And even when he wasn't gambling, his mind was still at the table—chasing, calculating, losing.

That email lit a fuse in me.

I sat there reading it, seething. Thinking—you stupid motherfucker.

You had me. You had a son. You had a chance to make sure someone never had to feel this way. And now, here you are, drowning in the same loneliness you gifted me my whole goddamn life.

From June to January, I buried myself in work. Reconnected with Brian. We were growing close again. Texting. Talking. Showing up.

Then Brian's mom got cancer.

She was everything to him. His North Star. His heart.

I watched him spiral—balancing fear and love and dread and work. I tried to show up for him the way he'd shown up for me. Quiet presence. Honest encouragement.

And I kept grinding.

Keto started working. The weight started falling. The wins kept stacking. But in the back of my mind, that voice wouldn't go quiet.

Any day now… Any day now, he's going to die.

And it's always been you who had to make it work.

I hated it. I hated the situation. I hated the grief. I hated the guilt. I hated myself.

And somewhere inside that hate, something new took root.

The day after my 35th birthday, the phone rang again. Just like it had the year before.

This time, it was his wife—Jerry.

"He's on hospice now. It's any day. If you have anything left to say, now's the time."

I told Chidley.

"Leave, Dan," he said. "Work will be here when you get back."

I texted my old boss.

She said the same.

Melissa looked at me and nodded.

So I packed a bag.

Got in the car.

And drove to Rapid City—not to rebuild anything.

But to say something permanent.

Goodbye.

32

The Drive to Closure

The drive from my place to Rapid City was fourteen hours.

Fourteen fucking hours of asphalt, silence, and thought. I could've flown, sure—but a last-minute round trip to Rapid was going to cost over seven hundred dollars, and no part of me wanted to throw that kind of money at something I didn't even want to do. Besides, I needed the time. I needed space to think. To prepare.

It had been ten years since I'd seen him. I didn't know what he looked like anymore. Not really. Not frail. Not dying. I needed to brace myself for that. I'd seen that look before, and it haunted me. I didn't want to flinch when I walked into that room.

During the drive, I reached out to the few people who had stayed close. Real ones. Brian picked up—he always did. Even though he was working, he made the time. Told me to call again if I needed to. Melissa and I talked back and forth. She kept me grounded with updates from home— London and Kingston being their usual wild, chaotic selves. Running her ragged. Reminding me that life still existed back home, waiting for me to return.

And then came the memories.

Every rest stop, every empty mile—old flashes of childhood started playing behind my eyes. Arcade games at Aladdin's Castle. Sitting on bleachers at the dirt track while he raced his hobby stock car around in slow, pointless circles. The man never won—maybe once, with a trophy to prove it—but he kept going. Probably just another form of gambling disguised as control.

And as I drove, my thoughts drifted to Diane.

God, she would've been so fucking disappointed in how it all turned out between us. She fought so hard to keep us connected. Always yelling at him to show up. "Get off your ass and go play with him. Take him outside. Do something." But he always had a reason—work, exhaustion, needing to relax. Always some excuse.

That made me think of her even more.

I remembered her yelling at me to clean under my fingernails. The way she could see straight through me, even when I was a kid. Diane didn't give a shit about religion or appearances. I didn't have to perform to be loved. Didn't have to earn my place. With her, just being me was enough.

And then came the whiplash of realizing that with my dad, it was the opposite. I always had to earn it. I had to chase it. And after all that chasing, all that effort, it still ended the same way.

A fucking end.

I thought about everything we could've done—should've done—and didn't. And that fire started to burn. Burned with anger that he had a son and let the relationship rot. Burned with resentment that now, at the end, he expected me to show up. Me, the son he barely knew anymore, the son he walked away from, was supposed to carry the script.

Then I thought about my sons.

About the way I love them. Even the one who lives eight hours away—I show up. I started brainstorming new ways to make sure they'd never have to wonder. Never have to question if I gave a shit.

And then the anger turned inward.

By the time I got to Rapid City, I was wrecked.

I got a hotel and crashed for the night. And there I was again—in that city, alone, in a room that didn't feel like anything, just waiting to walk into a house and tell my dying father that everything was going to be okay… when we both knew it wasn't.

The next morning, I waited by the phone. Eventually, one of his sisters or his wife called. He was awake. I could come over.

The dynamic was weird. No offer to stay. No real welcome. Just, "Get a hotel. Be close." It wasn't about the money—it was the tone. Like I was just another item on their to-do list.

I went and when I walked into that house, I didn't see a man. I saw a shell.

He was half-conscious. Fading in and out. Drugged up. Bald.

He'd always had a full head of hair. Even when I started balding, I used to joke I must've pulled from the wrong genetic line because both he and my grandpa had great hair. But there he was— bald, pale, ghost-like. With a massive goatee, which was even stranger. Growing up, he could barely grow facial hair. He used to joke, "Didn't even start shaving till I was thirty-five. You'll be the same."

Annoyingly accurate.

Now, he looked like a version of someone I might've known in another life. Familiar but hollow. The man who was supposed to guide me was the man I was now helping cross the finish line.

We didn't talk. Couldn't. He was too far gone.

Then the meds kicked in deeper. The human body gets weird when it's dying. His body told him he had to shit, but he couldn't. Constipated. Confused. Restless. The side effects clashed like drunk drivers, every system shutting down one by one.

At one point, he blinked at me and said, "Oh hey… when'd you get here?"

I said, "Been here a couple hours."

He nodded. "Good… good." Then he reached for my forearm like he wanted help.

I helped him walk with a fucking walker, dragging one side like his inner compass had snapped. What should've been a thirty-second walk turned into twenty slow, painful minutes. He'd freeze mid-step, sway like a tree in the wind, nearly topple—and I just held him.

He was still big. Six-two. Broad frame. Still looked like he could pour concrete if his body wasn't betraying him.

His wife and sisters tried to help too. But it wasn't just his body breaking down—it was his brain. And the brain, when it's dying, gets mean.

He lashed out. Screamed. Swore. Called people names.

Didn't matter who you were—if you touched a nerve, he exploded. No filter. No buffer. Just pain ricocheting in every direction. I knew it was the meds. The cancer. But it still fucking hurt.

At one point, I brushed his leg by accident, and he snapped.

"What the fuck is your problem? Get the fuck out of here, man."

I bit my tongue so hard it nearly bled.

All I wanted to do was scream back. But I didn't.

Instead, I said, "That's on me. I'm sorry."

He drifted off again.

And I just sat there.

Staring at the ceiling. Wondering how the fuck you forgive someone who made your life a constant lesson in survival. How you give grace to the person who let you build your identity around abandonment.

How many times in this book have I had to restart my life?

How many times have I had to claw my way out alone?

He didn't have to disappear. He chose to. And now I was here. Giving him peace.

Was it the right thing to do? I still don't know.

What I do know is I'll probably never talk to most of his family again. Hell, I was barely seen as a living person, just "his son." Not Dan. Not Danny. I was just a fucking footnote in his obituary.

Melissa and I bonded years ago over the fact that neither of us carry our father's last names. That name dies with him. My kids won't even know it unless they go looking for it.

At one point, while he laid in his big chair, I laid my forearm on the arm rest beside him.

Said the things you're supposed to say when someone's slipping.

"You're good. I'm good. I've got a family. I'm okay. You don't need to hold on anymore."

I said it like it was a line from a movie because it felt like a movie. And from the corner of my eye, I saw someone—maybe his wife, maybe his sister—pull out a phone and take a photo.

That was our last moment. My closure. I wasn't coming back. Not for a funeral. Not for ashes. Not for anything.

He gave me life. That's it.

No co-sign. No safety net. No wisdom. No kindness. Just absence, silence, and shadows.

Everything I am, I built with my own two fucking hands.

And as I helped him limp to the bathroom, I realized—I was giving him what he never gave me.

That night I drove around the old neighborhood. Past the tiny shack we lived in. Still looked the same. Same big bushes out front. A few blocks from my old high school.

I tried to feel something.

I didn't.

The next morning, I sat with him a few more hours. Quiet. Still. Holding back every word I wanted to scream. Every apology I never got. Every scar I stitched myself.

Here's something people don't tell you: when a parent dies, it can trigger a regression. Not physically—but emotionally. Psychologically. You slip back into whatever age you were when the damage happened. And for me?

That's thirteen.

I left that morning. Packed my car. Started the fourteen-hour drive back to Illinois. Planned to stop in Sioux City to see the kids. I needed to hold them. Remind myself of who I was.

And as I walked out the door, he lifted his head. Struggled to speak. His voice was paper-thin.

"I love you, Danny."

I stopped in the doorway. I remembered the last time I left Rapid City and what he said to me. "Yep." I replied... I'm just kidding. I'm not that fucked up.

"I love you too, Dad."

That was it.
Closure.

Not clean. Not perfect. But mine.

I got in the car and drove.

Called Melissa. Talked to a few friends. Vented to my brother, Bobby, — told him how tired I was, how messed up everything felt, how alone I'd been through every damn death.

And my brother—he said something I'll never forget.

"Maybe you had to go through all this... so when the rest of us do, we'll know how to get through it."

Maybe.

33

Rage in the Rearview

There's a reason I've always resonated with Eddie Brock, the Marvel character that wears the Venom symbiotic suit.

Not just the chaos. Not just the duality of self. But the core wound—the ache of being a son with a father who never figured out how to be one. In the comics, Eddie's relationship with his dad was a raw, infected thing. Cold. Distant. Conditional. And it never got better. Then years later, when Eddie had his own son, Dylan, he wasn't much better. The cycle just kept spinning. Damage handed down like inheritance.

That's what makes stories like his hit different for me. Because I lived it. And I wasn't about to live it again.

I got back to Illinois and took a couple of days off work. Just to breathe. Just to fucking process.

Then, a few days later—February 15, 2023—my dad died.

His sisters reached out. His wife, Jerry, too. They let me know the funeral would be in Rapid City. Then they planned a second service in Sioux City, a celebration of life. Jerry started calling me, texting my mom, trying to get in touch. She wanted to know if I wanted to go through his things—some comics, maybe some guns, a keepsake or two. I ignored them all.

It was over.

There was nothing physical I needed. Nothing symbolic. No part of me wanted to pick through a dead man's leftovers and pretend it meant something. He hadn't given me anything in life. Why would I want scraps in death?

And I was angry.

Not loud. Not explosive. Just… simmering. Unrelenting. Like a low fire behind my ribs.

I didn't know where to put that anger. Didn't have a healthy container for it. Melissa didn't fully understand what I was going through—how could she? I barely understood it myself.

So the smallest shit would set me off.

She'd overlook something small, and I'd snap. Or I'd misread something she said and turn it into a personal slight. My tone sharpened. My patience evaporated. I was either smiling or storming. Joy or rage. No middle ground.

London's birthday came. Around that time, Brian's mom passed.

Cancer. Just like my dad.

They held a virtual service. I attended. It was beautiful. Honest. Full of grace. And there I was, trying to balance the grief I hadn't processed with my own dad, while supporting my best friend through his loss.

I gave Brian every piece of good advice I could think of:

"One step at a time. Or an hour. Or a minute. Sometimes even a second. Just breathe."

And I meant every word.

But I couldn't take any of it in for myself.

Because I was still just… angry.

And when anger simmers that long, everything becomes a target.

Economy? Target.
Capitalism? Target.
Religion? Target.
My job? My effort? My leadership?
All of it started to feel like cogs in some soulless machine.

The only thing that kept me going was making sure no one else had to feel the pressure I felt. So I worked. I strategized. I studied the data like a madman. I was sharper than I'd ever been. Smarter. Faster. And when I failed? I failed fast. Got up. Kept grinding.

Because if I stopped—even for a moment—the anger would catch me.

But I started slipping.

I stopped anticipating and started assuming. Confidence hardened into cockiness. I began to move in absolutes, convinced my way was the only way. Yet absolutes don't work in leadership—people aren't formulas to be solved or equations to balance. The human element matters most, and I was starting to lose sight of it.

Some employees thrived under pressure, embracing the relentless pace, growing in the heat. Others, though, couldn't keep up. They felt unheard and unseen. They needed clarity I wasn't providing. And whenever someone else stepped in with a different answer than mine, it chipped away at my credibility.

Without credibility, trust erodes. And when you're leading from afar, trust isn't just important— it's everything.

Slowly, things would slip through the cracks. The place didn't fall apart but the culture shifted. It went from being fun to a fog of tension with performance and results.

The one thing keeping us on top was that everyone was making money. We were top five in the country for one of the most critical metrics in 2023. On paper, we were winning. But behind the scenes, everything was fraying.

Right before—or maybe just after—Brian's mom's funeral, Melissa and I flew to Ireland.

We needed space. A reset. Just air.

We spent a week in Dublin. Drove across the country, coast to coast. Hit small towns. Shared pints with locals in dimly lit pubs. Ate real food. Laughed with strangers. Slept like the world couldn't find us for once.

And while we were in Ireland, we had this running joke—about how unlucky we were. All the shit we'd been through. All the pain. All the detours. And there we were, in the land of "luck," talking about how fitting it would be to get the word "Unlucky" tattooed on us. Something small. Something real. We settled on a three-leaf clover—not four. Because three is the kind you find when you're not looking. When you're just surviving.

We walked into a shop in Dublin and got matching tattoos "Unlucky" inked on the right side of our right hands. Permanent proof that luck had nothing to do with what we'd built. It was grind. Always grind.

The stereotype hit hard across the countryside. Everywhere we went it was the same outpouring of sympathy. Seriously, because we were Americans we had a stereotype.

"All work, no play."

"America? Sorry, you must be exhausted."

"America, where it's 3 months pay for an ambulance ride to hospital."

They weren't wrong.

At one pub, we met a bartender named John. Laid-back. Funny. Local. As we chatted, I asked about closing hours. It was close to 10 p.m.

"Got about thirty minutes," he said.

I asked, "But if the place fills up, you stay open, right?"

He shook his head. "Nope. I've got a life to get home to."

And he meant it.

Later, while I was in the bathroom, John turned to Melissa and said something that stuck.

"That man right there is going to work himself to death."

She had tears in her eyes when she told me. And she was right to.

Because John saw what most people didn't. He saw the grind—not just as hustle or ambition— but as survival. He recognized that I wasn't just chasing goals… I was outrunning something. Rage. Grief. Collapse. He could see that if the grind ever stopped—if the machine so much as stuttered—I would fall apart. The work wasn't just work. It was the rhythm that kept the rage in the rearview.

He knew. And deep down, I think I did too.

Not long after we got back from Ireland, we found out she was pregnant again.

That news hit me like jet fuel. I was already grinding, but now? I lit another fire. I was going to make damn sure our future was stable, secure, and supported.

That summer, fueled by the baby news and the pressure I carried like oxygen, the grind didn't stop. But something started to shift.

Some coworkers became friends. People started asking if I was okay—not just in passing, but like they meant it.

One day, I was late. Traffic. Chaos. I walked into work rattled and frayed.

A coworker asked, "Hey, you alright?"

I snapped. "I'm fine. Why does everyone keep asking?"

They backed off.

But later, another coworker at the time who would become one of my best friends, Ashley (yeah, a whole new Ashley) pulled me aside.

"You know we have to ask, right?" she said. "Because we care. You've always got so much on your plate. We just want to make sure you're okay."

And I felt like shit.

Because they didn't deserve that. None of them did. I wasn't mad at them. I was just… reacting.

Chidley joked later, "I'm not gonna ask if you're okay." But there was warmth in it. He'd become like a big brother. People joked he was like my dad. I hated that comparison—because I didn't know how to love my dad. But this guy? He gave a damn.

One day, I snapped at him too.

He caught it—not in a punishing way, not with a glare or a lecture. Just… noticed. A pause. A shift. The kind of moment when someone sees through the cracks you've been hiding.

"What's going on?" he asked.

And I broke. Not loudly. Not in some dramatic collapse. It wasn't a shouting match or a monologue. It was slow. Like a leak you can't plug. Words just slipped out, quiet but heavy.

"I just feel like you don't care. Like I'm just your workhorse. Like if I quit tomorrow, it wouldn't even matter."

253

I saw the disappointment in his eyes. Real hurt. And that made everything worse. Because I cared. I cared so fucking much. I'd just buried it beneath the rage and the performance, pretending I didn't.

Later, after the moment passed, I sat with it. And that's when it hit me—how much I didn't like myself. The thoughts I never spoke out loud, the ones that spun endlessly in my head when the world got quiet. I'm a failure. I'm an idiot. I'm a piece of shit. Those weren't things I said to anyone else. But I said them to myself. Daily. Like a loop. Like a curse.

Shortly after that, I went on paternity leave. Four months.

A chance to breathe. A chance to slow the hell down. To heal.

Melissa only got four weeks, so I stepped up. I handled the chaos—early mornings, long nights, laundry mountains, crying fits, diaper blowouts, tantrums in stereo. I took over. Not out of obligation, but because I needed to. For her. For me. For us.

We named our daughter Brighton. She came out fierce—red hair, lungs like a lion, biggest baby we'd ever had on Dec 15th, 2023. We call her Stu. And yeah, she actually answers to it.

The first time I held her, I made a silent promise: I will do better. I am better. But even in that moment, I knew I hadn't gotten to the root yet.

I had a therapist. We were digging deep—childhood trauma, injustice, abandonment. Rage at the people who could've stepped up and didn't. Rage at how many times I'd had to figure it out alone.

And I had this pattern—this reflex to say nothing when I needed help. To overthink it until I felt like asking was too much. Like I was too much.

One day, Chidley asked if I needed anything. I brushed it off with a shoulder shrug and a half-lie. He didn't buy it.

"You gotta stop doing that," he said.

And something cracked open. Again.

Not in a big, cinematic way—but in a quiet flood. Everything came pouring out. Fear. Shame. Grief. Anger. All of it. And he just listened.

That's when I saw it clearly for the first time.

Everything I hated in my father?

It lived in me too.

And if I didn't do the work—if I didn't break the cycle—I was going to pass that same shit down. Like a curse passed down in silence.

I started a whole different kind of grind.

Not for redemption. Not to be liked. Not for validation.

Because I had to.

For my wife.
For all my kids.
For my friends.

For the people I lead.
For myself.

I went on leave not just to rest, but to rebuild. To come back not just refreshed—

But rewired.

Because the rage in my rearview had followed me long enough.

And it was time to finally address it head on.

34
Digging for the Root

Paternity leave was supposed to be a time of peace. Four months at home—time with the kids, time with Melissa, time to help, support, reflect. I was there for the late nights and early mornings, the bottles and blowouts, the laughs and the kind of exhaustion that rewrites your nervous system. Melissa had only a short window before she had to return to work, and I made damn sure I was present when she did. I got the schedules down, managed the madness, kept everything moving like clockwork. On paper, it looked ideal.

But in the quiet moments? I was still mad. I kept thinking about my dad. Wondering if I was mad at him, mad at myself, or both. Wondering what all this anger was really about. Paternity leave gave me space—but it didn't give me peace. Not yet.

Still, there was good in it. There were days when I felt calm. Days where a quiet sense of hope started to build under all the noise. I told myself when I returned to work, I wouldn't just run on metrics and performance. I wanted to run on people. On feelings. On connection. I didn't want to be someone who made others feel like shit just because I hadn't worked out my own. I wanted to be someone who ran toward people's crisis—not away from it.

So when I returned, I felt focused. Clear. Then I sit down for a debrief with Chidley. While I was out, he had conducted a skip-level review—anonymous feedback from my team. I walked in expecting praise. I thought maybe, finally, they'd recognize the growth.

They didn't. The feedback was honest. Brutal. Unfiltered. There were real gaps in how I communicated, in how I carried myself, in how fast I moved without slowing down for others. And as much as I wanted to take it with grace and professionalism, the truth is—I unraveled. I was back in 2023, reacting instead of processing. Within days, I felt myself regressing into the version of me I'd worked so hard to leave behind. It crushed me.

I thought about how Chidley must have felt when I accused him of not caring about me—and how wrong I had been. How much that must've hurt. And now, here I was, getting a taste of that same disappointment. And it wrecked me. So I owned it. I stood the fuck up and owned it. It was like dusting off an old muscle memory—one I hadn't worked in too long. But I started showing up differently.

Keto was working. But so was the stress. So was the weight of the work. I dropped 120, maybe 130 pounds. I looked like a completely different person. Not the muscular version from before— just lean, wiry, unfamiliar. My walk changed. My tone softened. My presence was quieter now.

Instead of leading with numbers, I started leading with people. I asked how they were feeling— not just what they were selling. If I gave direction, I checked for clarity. I started doing random check-ins. "Hey, how are you today?" And when the answer was about work, I stopped them. "No, how are you? Your partner, your family, your life—how's that?" I didn't want anyone under my leadership to feel invisible.

When a manager complained about an underperforming employee, I didn't just ask for their sales numbers—I asked how they'd been acting. What their energy was like. If anything had changed. We didn't treat symptoms. We dug for roots.

And it worked. Fast. We started winning again. Morale climbed. People started getting promoted. Surveys came back with some of the best scores in the region. The culture shifted. The connection was real.

I started opening up more, letting pieces of my story come through when it made sense—grief, loss, growing up fast, raising siblings, losing my sons. People were stunned. "I had no idea," they'd say. "Me too," they'd whisper. That's when I remembered Diane's voice: Use your voice. So I did. Not to preach. But to connect. I stopped assuming. I started asking. I kept redirecting the same anger that used to burn me alive—but now I was pouring it into growth. Into change. Into leadership that actually meant something.

But it wasn't perfect. I still had moments. Still snapped. Still spiraled. Still let old patterns creep back in. The difference now? I caught myself. And others caught it too. One person even said, "I didn't know where that conversation was going at first, but damn, you pulled it back." The trick now was to stop myself before the words ever hit the air.

And while things were getting better at work—more intentional, more thoughtful—things at home were harder. I was doing to Melissa what I used to do to everyone else. Overreactions. Misinterpretations. Holding onto things out of context. Letting my own trauma turn molehills into mountains.

She didn't always understand what I needed—and I didn't explain it well. When my dad died, she admits now that she didn't know how much it would affect me. She didn't show up the "right" way—because I never showed her what that looked like. And that spiraled us. For a while.

At home I was beginning to get tangled in a whole new yet familiar grief. London was getting older. And she wasn't talking like we'd hoped. At first, we thought it was a phase. But eventually it became clear—this wasn't just a delay. She's nonverbal. She has autism. And all the optimism I'd been projecting outward started to collapse inside me.

I had imagined us talking over coffee one day. I pictured telling her what she meant to me. I imagined her knowing—really knowing—how she saved me after her brothers died. I thought someday, I'd look her in the eyes and thank her for giving me a reason to keep going. Now… I don't know if that day will ever come.

And that's a grief no one prepares you for. You don't lose your daughter—but you lose the version of her you thought you'd get to know. You lose conversations. Milestones. A kind of closeness you'd imagined. And it breaks you in ways that don't show up in pictures.

Still, I kept going. I applied for a promotion. I didn't get it. But I didn't spiral. I called Chidley and said exactly how I felt. "I really thought I'd done enough to show I was the guy." And we had a real conversation. One hour later, I hosted a flawless visit with a VP and a senior director. Why? Because I used my voice. I took a page out of Diane's book.

That year, I ended ranked number one in the entire company for one of the most important metrics we track. And I did it without pushing performance like it was life or death. We looked at data every day—but we obsessed over strategy. Behavior. Mindset. Connection. The numbers followed.

The work was healing. But home still had cracks. Melissa was struggling. Walking on eggshells. Afraid to say the wrong thing. And I didn't make it easy. My tone. My intensity. The emotional whiplash—it wore her down.

And then there was Brian. I kept trying to reach out. Set up time. Stay close. I'd get the occasional message—"Hey, how are you?"—but it always felt distant. I bought gifts and mementos and asked to meet up. I waited. But it felt like water slipping through my fingers.

Then one day, Melissa told me she had reached out to him herself. Just to see if he could find time for me. Because she saw how much I needed it—a break, a friend, someone who saw me beyond all the roles. But by then, we had no one to help with the kids. No date nights. No lifelines.
I lived at work or at home. That was it.

So I built a routine. Wake up. Make breakfast. Clean. Drop the kids. Work. Grind. Come home. Reset. Repeat. It was so dialed in, so automatic, that any ripple—any deviation—felt like a threat. Because structure meant control. And control kept the grief away.

Then, on Thanksgiving, Brian texted me. Simple: "Happy Thanksgiving. Spending time with friends." He mentioned his new girlfriend like I should've already known.

I hadn't.

And it hit me like a knife. How the fuck would I know?

I spiraled. Didn't take it out on anyone. But I was done. I couldn't do it again—not the slow dying of another friendship

261

while I stood still, waiting. I thought about Travis. And I got scared.

I wrote Brian a message. Poured it out. Told him I couldn't do it anymore. That I wasn't going to relive this kind of slow loss again. I had already lived a lifetime of communicating through letters and didn't want to relive that through texting as an adult. I wasn't going to be the one holding space for someone who didn't hold any for me.

He responded. Said he'd been trying in his own way. Said he needed time to process what I'd said. He made points when he had reached out a few times. That he thought I was good. He apologized.

But I was already done waiting. It had been two years of chasing, hoping, and wishing to have a friendship more than being pen pals. I never replied. And he never reached out again. I told myself it was closure. That I was protecting my peace. That drawing the line was the strong thing to do. But truthfully? It was devastating. Another slow death of something I once believed in. Another bond slipping through my fingers, not with fire—but with silence.

And just as I felt myself retreating again, slipping back into that place where I shut the world out, where I folded into my own silence like armor—something happened. My two best friends. Ashley and Adam, real ones. They saw it happening. Saw me shrinking back. Saw the door starting to close—and they didn't let it. They didn't text. Didn't wait for the right moment. They showed up. In person. They looked me in the eye and owned their part. And in their eyes, I saw it—that same look I'd seen in Melissa. In Chidley. In myself. Disappointment. Not in who I was, but in how I was hiding.

And it rocked me. That's when I realized—I was doing it again. Pushing people away not because they failed me, but because I was afraid of losing them. Because if I walked away first, at least it would be my choice. That had always been the pattern. My cycle. My shield. And I knew, right then, it had to break.

A trip to Puerto Rico came next—a work incentive for top performers. Melissa came with me. And when we landed, I felt it immediately. That quiet fork in the road. I could show up to celebrate and hide behind charm, or I could show up real. Present. Accountable. No masks. No armor.

I thought back to something Travis once asked me, under a full moon while we smoked: "Are you really who you want to be, or just the version that makes everyone else happy?" That question cracked something open. Not all at once. But enough to let the light in.

So I dug. Dug into the past. Into the parts of myself I'd buried so deeply I forgot they were still alive. I dug into the version of me that first learned to perform. The moment I stopped feeling seen. The moment I started building walls.

Chidley once said to me—after I called myself a piece of shit without even realizing I'd said it aloud—"You need to learn how to give yourself some grace."

I didn't know how. But I started trying.

Because here's the truth: I hated my dad for what he did. For what he didn't do. Because he had time—plenty of time—to own his shit and do better. And he didn't. And for all my effort not to become like him, I started seeing pieces of myself in his shadow. Especially in how I treated Travis. Especially in what I didn't say until it was too late.

And that's what finally broke me.

Because the real wound wasn't just what my dad did to me.

It was what I had done, too.

And now? Now I had to figure out how to forgive myself.

Because without grace, there is no healing. And without healing, you end up dragging your past through every room you walk into—pulling everyone you love into it with you.
But I don't want to drag anyone anymore.

I want to grow.

So I started working—really working—on how to give myself grace.

Because once I can do that?

Maybe I can finally give it to everyone else, too.

35
Concrete Foundations

My dad spent his life in concrete.

He was a foreman. Construction ran through his veins the way adrenaline surges before a fight— steady, cold, necessary. He could lay a foundation with his eyes closed. Knew the right mix, the right weight, how to read the weather and the wind and know if the pour would hold. Concrete was his art. It was his medium, the thing he could control.

And maybe that's what makes all of this so fucking ironic— because after he died, I started the opposite journey. While he mastered construction, I became a student of deconstruction. Not just physically. Not buildings. Me. My life. My foundations. I ripped up every piece of rebar and mental framing I had, trying to figure out what was underneath. What was holding it all up. Why the walls were crooked. Why I reacted the way I did. Why I kept ending up back in the same cycles.

I never really knew who I was—just who I was supposed to be. The achiever. The son. The Christian. The husband. The leader. The example. Every role came with a set of labels, and I wore them like armor, not realizing that armor eventually rusts and caves in. Somewhere in all that pretending, I lost myself. Or maybe I never had a chance to meet myself to begin with.

Remembering Travis asking me who I was planted a seed. And over time, it bloomed into this relentless need to dig—to understand myself, to stop being angry all the damn time, to stop living like a grenade with the pin already pulled, just waiting for the wrong word—or the wrong silence—to set me off.

Because here's what I learned: if I don't know how to give myself grace, I sure as hell can't give it to anyone else. If I keep dragging people into my past, holding them accountable for old ghosts they don't even know are haunting me, I'll keep everyone around me stuck too. I'll freeze them in a moment of time that only I remember. And that's not fair.

So, I started digging. Not for answers. For origins. I wasn't mad that my dad died, I was mad at him. And that makes no sense, right? He's gone. It's over. Nothing more he can do. It's permanent. So why the hell was I so mad?

Then I remembered my 13th birthday party. Surprise party. All my friends, decorations, cake. My dad and Diane showed up—but he didn't even get out of the car. She came up, smiled, gave me a hug. He stayed in the car. Waved. That was it. A half-assed hello from behind glass, from a man who had every opportunity to be more—and didn't take it. And that memory cracked something open.

Because the night I didn't call Travis? That's all I did. I waved. Sat in my car. And watched. I didn't get out. I didn't show up. I didn't grab him by the shoulders and tell him I loved him. I became the thing I hated. I became my dad. And I couldn't fucking live with that. Because Travis? He always showed up for me.

So now I'm mad at myself. Alone. And isolated. And I start spiraling, whispering shit to myself like, you're a piece of shit, over and over again until it becomes law. Until it echoes loud enough that others start believing it too.

I was stuck between grief and guilt. Between memory and regret. Between being the man, I thought I was and the man I feared I had become. But I started realizing something else, too— Travis wasn't just my best friend. He was everyone's. His death didn't just wreck me. It wrecked rooms full of people. He was that guy. The one who made you feel seen when the rest of the world looked away.

And it hit me—how selfish I was being. Like I was trying to own all the grief, like I was the only one who lost something. And that wasn't right. So I took a step forward. One. Small. Step. I started to accept that he was gone. Not move on. Just accept. And it was the first step toward grace.

And grace? That's a whole new muscle to build.

I started seeing how quick I was to assume. How fast I leapt from anticipation to assumption, then frustration. I'd think, if you know me, why don't you know this about me already? But people aren't mind readers, and I never said anything out loud.

Like when my mom came to visit. We went to this kid's museum, and I was tense the whole time. She was on her phone instead of playing with the grandkids. Then she suggested making chicken Alfredo for dinner, and I told her that I didn't like it. Never had. She made it anyway. Hours later, I didn't touch the plate. She pushed. I snapped. "How the fuck would you not know I don't like this? I'm your oldest son!" It wasn't about the food. It was about never feeling seen. Never feeling heard. And with Travis gone—the one person who always did see me—I felt invisible again. And when I feel invisible, I lash out.

That's the thing about unhealed grief—it seeps into everything. Even the way you argue.

I remember one of my closest friends telling me during an argument, "We're not perfect. And neither are you. And this won't work without grace." That line gutted me. Because she was right. And it wasn't just about her. It was about everyone I'd pushed away. Everyone I'd assumed would always be there—Mark. Kiley. Brian. All these people I thought were permanent. And now? Gone. Like ghosts who never even said goodbye.

But then there's the other side. The people who do show up. My wife. My kids. But let's be real teenagers talk when they want. And toddlers? Toddlers are just tiny maniacs you're trying to keep from swallowing batteries or jumping off the fridge. They're not emotional support. They're chaos with arms. And it's not their job to fix my loneliness. It's not a child's job to carry your grief.

That's on me.

And even with Melissa—my rock—she's got her own life, her own load. I can't put all this weight on her shoulders and expect her not to buckle. That's not love. That's smothering.

So, I started looking for the root. Which took me all the way to basic. A decision. A question. Why did I believe Ashley and make that call to Travis?

The truth? Because I believed Ashley over him. I chose her family. Because her family felt safe. Stable. Like a place I wouldn't be abandoned. When my grandpa died and Travis was gone, her family was there. And I trauma bonded. I clung to them like a life raft.

But Travis' family? They would've chosen me. If I'd just chosen them back.

That's the part that wrecks me.

And this whole deconstruction—it's not a self-help exercise. It's hell. But I'm doing it because I owe it to myself. I owe it to Travis. I owe it to the man I want to be. I owe it to the kids who need me not just present, but whole.

I owe it to the memory of the people who taught me better—my grandpa, Diane, Travis— because they'd be pissed if they saw the way I was letting this destroy me from the inside out.

And I'm still learning.

I'm learning to pause. To check my tone. To stop assuming. To trust more. To speak up. To stop whispering "you're a piece of shit" into the mirror and start saying something else. Something true. Something better.

Because I wasn't the man I wanted to be.

But I can still become him.

And that starts by pouring a new foundation.

Not from concrete.

From grace.

And here's what cracked that foundation open even more: after he died, I started digging through family records on Ancestry. Just trying to understand. Fill in blanks. I found out he had an older brother—one I never knew about. A baby who died. A death that his father—my grandfather— was arrested for. A piece of our family history completely erased. Buried. Never once spoken about.

What kind of grief does a man carry when that's how his childhood starts?

What kind of trauma did he keep welded shut, deep in the pit of his chest, behind layers of poured concrete and stubborn pride?

I remembered something then. Before the cancer diagnosis, before the fallout, there was a day he called me. Jerry—his wife—was sitting next to him. He was giddy. Nervous. Proud.

"Hey, Danny! I just proposed to Diane, and she said yes!"

And I remember thinking—did he mean to say Jerry and accidentally call her Diane? Or was it something else? A moment of vulnerability trying to sneak out in disguise?

Maybe that was his way of reaching for something familiar. Something soft. Something he never had the words for.

Because my dad was strong with concrete. But using his voice? That was always harder than any cement he ever laid.

And now I'll never get to ask him what he was really holding in.

But I know what I'm not holding anymore. I'm not holding silence.

I'm holding grace. And building something new from it.

36
Living with an Uninvited Guest

Grief didn't come knocking on my door one day—it's always been here. In the stale air of hospital rooms. In the clatter of silverware after someone leaves the table for good. In the silence that follows laughter that didn't last. It was in the way voices changed when bad news came, in the heaviness of hugs that lingered too long. I didn't meet grief. I was born into it.

At two years old, my uncle Jeff was murdered, and that one act detonated everything around it. My family didn't get a chance to rebuild before another wave came. The grief of losing Chad. The grief of a marriage dissolving. The grief of a business and a future slipping away. I was raised not with hope, but with heaviness. It settled in early. Before I ever had words for it.

That's why, for most of my life, I didn't think grief went away—because I never knew it could. It wasn't something you moved past. It was something you buried, layered under expectations and silence. To me, that was normal. That was life. But later—when I had the tools, the language, and the willingness—I started to understand that grief doesn't vanish, and it doesn't stay quiet. It's not something you defeat. It's something you learn to walk with.

Like Diane once told me, "You have to live in the good memories to keep them alive." I didn't fully understand what she meant at the time. But now I do. Because that's what grief becomes— it turns memories into bridges, not barriers. It teaches you that the ache never fully leaves. It just becomes part of the terrain. You stop trying to erase it. You just learn how to carry it better.

Every time I go back to Sioux City to see my kids, it rises. The memories of Travis. The ghost of all that we were and all we didn't get to be. You don't ever fully outrun it—you just learn how to walk beside it. And over time, grief gave me a gift—something I never expected.

That insight isn't just personal—it's backed by research. A study published in the Journal of Affective Disorders found that individuals who processed grief through meaning-making—reframing their loss in a way that gave purpose or perspective—reported lower levels of depression and greater psychological resilience. In other words, when you find a way to live with grief, rather than fight it, you unlock something deeper than just survival. You begin to build strength.

When I read that unresolved grief can manifest as anxiety, anger, or detachment... it felt like someone had written my biography in a peer-reviewed journal. According to the American Psychological Association, this is common. Suppressed grief doesn't fade. It festers. That's why so many of us walk around with unseen scars—lashing out or shutting down. Not because we're cold, but because we've been carrying a weight too heavy, for too long, with no room to set it down.

I didn't want to keep carrying that weight alone. So I started doing what I could to hand pieces of it to others—not to burden them, but to make space for connection. I stopped trying to act like I was invincible. And that act? That's what almost killed me.

The truth is, grief doesn't just live in your head—it settles into your body. Research from Harvard Medical School shows how early exposure to trauma can get wired into your nervous system, shaping how you process emotion and physically carry pain. That's what happened to me. I didn't just grieve—I wore it. After my dad passed, I lost another 70 pounds. That brought my total weight loss to 140. It wasn't from lifting or running or some clean macro plan. It was stress. Burnout. Grief compounding on top of grief. And my body, like my mind, was trying to survive it the only way it knew how—by shrinking.

And I didn't understand for a long time that grief doesn't stop with the person who dies. Psychologists call it "secondary loss." You don't just lose the person. You lose the future you imagined with them. You lose traditions, conversations, routines. You lose parts of yourself that only made sense in their presence. I lost versions of my identity every time someone left.

So when people tried to comfort me with, "Everything happens for a reason," or "God has a plan," it didn't land. It didn't soothe. It stung. According to research from the University of Memphis, phrases like that—while often meant with kindness— can actually deepen isolation. They imply closure where there isn't any. They push grief away instead of sitting in it. Grief doesn't want explanation. It just wants presence.

Ironically, grief gave me the best perspective I've ever had.

For a long time, everything was gray. Numb. Dead behind the eyes. But when I started living with grief instead of under it, something shifted. The world didn't just brighten—it deepened. Breezes hit different. Grass looked greener. The blue in the sky had texture again. Even silence wasn't as sharp—it became space instead of absence.

And on the hard days, I open my mouth and speak. I reach out. I don't wait for someone to notice I'm spiraling. Because I want the people I've lost to live through me. I want their story to echo in the way I keep going.

Grief changed how I see others, too. I don't want anyone else to feel the way I've felt. That's why I ask people how they're really doing—not to fill silence, but to pull them out of it. I mix humor with honesty because sometimes laughter is the only rope long enough to pull you out of a dark place. I've learned that when someone shares their story, they start to recognize themselves again. Grief tries to erase identity. Storytelling brings it back.

Look, if you're reading this and you're in the thick of it—let me be clear. I won't tell you this is all part of some divine plan. I won't tell you God needed another angel. I won't tell you that everything happens for a reason. Because those words, no matter how well-meaning, strip the chaos out of what you're experiencing.

And grief is chaos.

It's random. It's cruel. It's real. And it doesn't need your permission to take up space in your life.

No one should be forced to endure grief just to grow. You can evolve without suffering. But if you are in it—then the only thing to do is survive it.

One day at a time.
Or an hour.
Or a minute.
Or even a second.

Whatever it takes.

Because you don't stop. The world won't wait for you to catch your breath. It keeps spinning. And you do too.

If I could get through everything I've been through—if I could learn to stop running from it, to sit in it, to walk beside it without letting it swallow me—then you can too.

You're not alone.

Even if it feels like you are.

Grief will always be an uninvited guest.
But you don't have to let it take over the house.

Set it a seat at the table.
Acknowledge it.
And then keep living anyway.

37

When Grief Isn't Yours, But Still Lives in the Room

There's a brutal irony in grief—how easy it is to forget that someone else's pain doesn't need your explanation. It needs your presence.

That's something I didn't learn in a book. I learned it in real time, through missteps, silence, and saying the wrong shit more than once.

Because here's what I know now: the worst thing anyone can say to a grieving person is that their pain is part of some divine strategy. That there's a reason for it. That God has a plan.

When people said that to me, after the boys, after Travis, after Diane, it didn't land as comfort— it landed like a punch.

So what? God needed my baby boys to die, but lets some guy down the block addicted to chaos keep popping out ten healthy kids? You're telling me that's the plan? You're not helping me cope—you're giving me someone to blame.

A study from the Journal of Religion and Health confirms that religious platitudes like "God has a plan" often increase emotional distancing and spiritual confusion in people experiencing complicated grief—especially those who don't already hold strong religious convictions. It's like slapping a faith-flavored Band-Aid on a deep wound and wondering why it doesn't heal.

Know your audience. Know their heart. Or just shut the fuck up and sit beside them.

Because what meant the most to me in my darkest moments wasn't words at all—it was presence. It was the people who reached out without being asked. The text that came out of nowhere. The friend who showed up without needing a reason. Because when you're grieving, you already feel invisible. When someone steps into that space with care, it cuts through the fog.

What I wanted—what I needed—was for someone to say: "Tell me about them."

Not "It's going to be okay."
Not "They're in a better place."
Just: "Tell me."

Tell me about your sons. Tell me about Travis. Tell me what you dreamed about that didn't happen. Let's talk about the pain and the hope, the love and the loss. That's the thing—grief doesn't want to be solved. It wants to be witnessed.

And yet, even after a lifetime of living with grief, I found myself stumbling when it was someone else's turn.

When Brian's mom passed, I didn't know how to show up. I didn't know what to say. I was so deep in my own shit— processing my dad's decline, feeling angry, confused, juggling pressure at work—I froze. He was grieving, and I was over here unsure how to navigate it, especially while watching him step into a new relationship.

And that hit me harder than I expected.

Not just because he was moving forward, but because I wasn't. I was stuck. I felt like the world was accelerating around me while I was still trying to make sense of what I'd lost. I didn't know how to be present for his grief while feeling like mine hadn't even found its own footing. And deep down, I was terrified— terrified that I'd be just another person who let someone down in their grief, the way I had felt let down too many times in mine.

It cracked something open.

But there was one moment—a phone call I'll never forget—that showed me what presence really looks like when grief isn't yours, but it's living in the room.

Josh called me. His best friend, Nate—someone who, when they stood next to each other, looked like me and Travis had been reincarnated—was gone. Killed. And my brother? He was in pieces. There wasn't even language for the kind of grief pouring out of him.

I remember the way Bobby talked to me afterward, and I remember how quickly I kicked into motion. Not to fix it. But because I know Josh. And I knew this grief. I knew what it could do. I started calling people, giving advice, offering ways to show up. I wasn't guessing—I was speaking from the inside out. Because I knew what it was like to be him. I was him once.

I remember telling our brother, Bobby, "I know you think your way is right, but I'm literally telling you what he would need— because we're the same."

But most of the people around him didn't listen. And I let it go. I had said what I needed to say.

Months later, Josh and I sat down. He asked if I thought he was out of his mind or if I had been on the money. I'll never forget what he said next: "You were one of the few who showed up exactly how I needed. You didn't try to fix it. You were just there."

That's it.

That's the whole thing.

Grief doesn't ask you to save someone. It asks you to stay.

One of the biggest myths people believe about grief is that it ends. That there's a time frame. A clean-up date. That grief fades with distance, or that the level of pain you're allowed to feel depends on how "important" that person was, or how old they were.

Bullshit.

I lost Diane—my stepmom—but she was my mother in every way that mattered. Still, when I told people, their reactions were different than if I had said "my mom died."

Same thing with my great-grandparents. People think if someone dies at 85, it shouldn't hurt as much as losing someone at 15.

But grief isn't mathematical. It's relational.

The Journal of Loss and Trauma backs this up. Their findings show that the perceived closeness of a relationship—not the person's age or title—predicts the depth of grief. In other words, the more someone was part of your soul, your routine, your identity—the deeper the loss.

So instead of assuming, ask.

Ask what they meant to them.
Ask what made them unforgettable.
Ask what their absence now echoes in your day-to-day life.

Because that's what I do now.

When someone around me is hurting, I ask questions. If they're open, I listen. If they're not ready, I sit beside them and let the silence say, I see you.

I stopped assuming I knew what to say.

I just ask:

- What were your dreams with them?
- What memories keep surfacing?
- What made them them?
- What about their loss is haunting you?

Sometimes, it's not about talking. Sometimes it's about sitting still and being the one person who isn't afraid to face the sadness with them.

We're not here to fix each other's grief. We're here to witness it. To say, "You're allowed to feel every inch of this, and I'll sit with you while you do."

At work, this mindset changed everything.

When someone underperformed, I didn't just look at numbers. I asked why. Why now? Why today? Why this person?

What grief aren't they naming? What storm are they walking through quietly?

Because when your eyes are open to grief, you start to see how many people are carrying it invisibly.

And when you become curious—genuinely curious—you start helping people find the root. Not just the symptom.

I've learned that you don't need to fix someone to help them heal.

You just need to give them the dignity of being seen.

Grief will always be in the room.

But we can be in the room too.

38
When the House Is Heavy

There's a brutal irony in grief—how easy it is to forget that someone else's pain doesn't need your explanation. It just needs your presence. I didn't learn that from a book or a podcast. I learned it sitting across from Melissa on nights when the house felt heavier than our words. When she needed answers, and I gave her silence.

Being a partner in your darkest moments is a test no one trains you for. It's not something you read about or plan for—it just happens. And when it does, it's suffocating.

Grief doesn't just make you sad. It makes you heavy. And when you're that heavy, you stop moving. You isolate. And in a relationship, when one of you stops moving, the whole foundation starts to shift.

For a long time, I was buried under the weight of everything—loss, stress, self-loathing, performance pressure, unresolved trauma. And Melissa? She was carrying her own shit too. Her own grief. Her own exhaustion. But when I went silent, when I didn't speak up or explain where I was mentally, emotionally, spiritually—I forced her to play a guessing game.

That's not partnership. That's slow suffocation.

I realized that by keeping my struggles inside, I was making her carry the confusion, the pressure, the emotional labor. I was handicapped by grief, yes—but my silence was toxifying everything we'd built. We had always seen ourselves as "us against the world," but my isolation was isolating her too. And if she slipped into a dark place too, while I was still stuck in mine— what the hell would that do to our kids?

So I started talking. Not with eloquence. Not always calmly. But I began saying things like, "I think I'm slipping again." I started flagging bad days instead of pretending they didn't exist. Because when you love someone, you don't shield them by going quiet. You protect them by inviting them into the fight.

I owned my shit.

And that ownership saved us.

There was one moment, during an argument, where Melissa said something that stopped me cold: "What would you do if a man ever spoke to one of your daughters the way you're speaking to me right now?"

I don't remember the fight. I don't remember the topic. But I remember that question. Because it made me look at myself in the mirror and flinch.

Words are weapons. And when you're passionate, articulate, and hurting—they can be nuclear.

I've always had a way with words. I can make people feel seen. But if I'm not careful, I can also make people feel small. And realizing I had made my wife cry with words—not once, but multiple times—shook me. Not just her. My friends. People I cared about. People who showed up when I couldn't even show up for myself.

It was unacceptable. And I knew it.

So I started tracking the source of that anger. Not just to manage it—but to dismantle it. Because anger doesn't have to be the villain. But it does need to be reined in before it becomes one.

In that process, I realized my kids were teaching me what forgiveness looks like—pure, fast, unconditional. When I made mistakes, they didn't hold it over me. They wanted hugs. Connection. Presence. And when you slow down and really see your kids, you see the world through a different lens.

Everything is a first to them.

The first falling leaf. The first snowflake. The first scraped knee. The first time they feel pain and realize it's part of life.

And in their awe, in their joy, in their simple wonder—you're reminded that this world is still a beautiful place, even if you've forgotten.

Kids aren't crutches. They're not there to heal us. But they do teach us how to heal if we're willing to pay attention.

And one day, if they go through grief like I have—I want them to have a playbook. Not a perfect one. But a real one. I want them to remember how I owned my darkness, how I didn't use them as an emotional crutch, how I showed them what it looks like to process pain without inflicting it.

I want to give them a fighting chance.

As for Melissa? We both thought we were near the end. We didn't talk about it while it was happening, but after the smoke cleared, we admitted it: we both had thought it was over.

She felt like nothing she said or did would ever be enough. That every word would be twisted. That I was fundamentally unhappy being married to her.

And honestly, I thought the same about her.

But then I slowed down. I started asking for context instead of assuming I already knew the ending to a sentence she hadn't even finished. I started listening. And when I did, everything began to shift.

We made it because I changed. Because I decided to change. Because I realized that love doesn't survive by default. It survives by choice, effort, and accountability.

And if my kids ever read this—if one day you're old enough to pick this book up and ask yourself who your dad really was—I want you to remember this:

Grief is brutal. It's confusing. And it hurts more than I can explain.

But it's not something you ever have to face alone.

You need to speak up when you're hurting. Not everyone will understand—but the right people will try.

Set boundaries. Protect your peace. Don't let people convince you they'll show up when they keep proving they won't. But don't close the door on those who want to help just because others failed you.

Ask questions. Be curious. Know who's really in your corner. And be honest about what you need.

And if I'm not here when that moment comes—if I'm not around to walk you through your pain—then I hope everything I've written, everything I've lived, will be enough to guide you.

Because maybe, just maybe, I had to walk through all of it so that you don't have to walk through it alone.

39

The Lie They Never Warn You About

I used to believe the biggest win in leadership was helping people make money.

That was the lie.

A lie rooted in good intentions, sure—but a lie, nonetheless.

For a long time, I thought when you help your team get results, and they'll follow you anywhere. Give them the playbook. Show them the path. Celebrate their wins. Drive performance. Get them paid.

And for a few, that worked. The ones wired like me—obsessed with growth, hungry for the hustle, addicted to the grind—they thrived. They loved the speed, the precision, the push. But leadership isn't about some of your people. It's about all of them.

And I didn't see that—not fully—until it was too late.

Because while I was sprinting forward, driven by purpose and strategy, I left some of them behind. I assumed they saw what I saw. Felt what I felt. I assumed they felt seen. But they didn't. They felt left out, unheard, invisible. Because what I thought was lifting them up was actually burying them under my pace.

Leadership isn't about who can keep up with you. It's about how you slow down and meet people where they are.

The Center for Creative Leadership found that one of the top reasons employees disengage isn't poor pay or lack of training—it's a feeling of being unseen and undervalued. I wasn't failing to lead—I was failing to notice. And that's when the trust started to break.

What Empathy Actually Looks Like

Leading with empathy is not a checkbox. It's not asking someone, "What motivates you?" or
"What would you do with a big commission check?" That's corporate theater. That's just noise.

Empathy is saying: Tell me about your story.

It's ditching the robotic scripts and showing up as a human being. No jargon. No masks. Just real talk.

When I lead with empathy, I try to understand the emotion behind the behavior. I ask myself what pressure this person is carrying, what memory they might be reliving, or what invisible weight they're shouldering today. Empathy is about adjusting—not expecting someone to rise to where you are but instead meeting them at their level and lifting together.

A 2021 report from Catalyst showed that leaders who demonstrate empathy are more likely to drive engagement, reduce burnout, and increase employee retention. No surprise there. Empathy isn't soft—it's strategic. It's the only leadership trait that impacts performance, trust, and loyalty in equal measure.

The Moment I Knew I Had Earned It Back

There was a moment I'll never forget. A turning point that didn't come from a metric—it came from a conversation. One of my managers, someone I had clashed with early on, called me out of the blue. We hadn't always seen eye to eye. I had come in hot— moving fast, too fast. I labeled her context as excuses and pushed her hard, too hard. It got to the point where she nearly quit.

But then we slowed down. We listened. We talked. We saw each other not as roles, but as people. And that changed everything.

One day, she called me—not to talk about business or goals— but to say: "Dan, I don't know what to do. One of my employees is having a really hard time. He lost his friend to suicide. He's snapping, he's off. His numbers are down. He's not himself. Can you talk to him? Maybe he'll open up to you."

That call said everything.

The trust she placed in me allowed me to reach out to him—not as a manager, but as a person. We talked. We connected. And today, that employee is one of my top performers. Not because I pushed harder—but because someone made space for him to be seen and heard.

Then came more calls:

"My family member was just diagnosed with brain cancer—can I talk to you?"

"My spouse just left me, and I don't know what to do."

"Can you call my rep? They didn't get the promotion and they're spiraling."

That's when I knew the trust was back. Not because I said the right things, but because I showed up the right way. Because people started to believe in what I believed—that we weren't just here to hit numbers. We were here to help people change their lives.

I heard my own mantras coming back to me: "We work to help people make life-changing money." They weren't just my words anymore—they were our words. That's when you know your leadership is working. When belief becomes culture.

But I also know what it feels like to lose that trust.

It broke when people started talking about me but not to me. When concerns went up the ladder or out the door but never landed in my inbox. That's when I realized: you don't always lose trust in a bang. Sometimes it slips out through silence.

Being Real Without Being Reckless

Leading with empathy isn't always safe—especially in corporate environments that still reward toughness over truth. There's risk in vulnerability. You risk being misunderstood. You risk being labeled "soft." But I'd rather risk being misread than lead from a place that never shows anyone what real care looks like.

That's the balance: real and responsible. Vulnerable and accountable. Human and high standard.

People say, "Be authentic," like it's a switch you flip. But being real and responsible is a daily balancing act. I'm 100% myself, but I'm also self-aware. That means I can't drop a casual "fuck" in front of frontline employees or customers—no matter how authentic it might be in the moment.

But caring? Caring is professional.

That same VP I talked about earlier in the book said something that stuck with me: "If you're not holding someone accountable, you're lying to them."

And she was right.

If you really care about your people, you don't keep letting them fall short. You don't pat them on the back while they self-sabotage. And you don't let yourself off the hook either.

That moment changed me. Because it wasn't just about holding them accountable—it was about holding myself accountable, too. I stopped lying. I stopped excusing my shortcuts. I owned my shit.

And everything shifted.

In fact, studies by TalentSmart show that 90% of top performers have high emotional intelligence, and those with higher EQ earn an average of $29,000 more per year than their lower EQ peers. Emotional intelligence isn't fluff—it's impact. It drives connection, which drives performance.

That data backed what I was starting to feel: the more honest I got with myself, the more human I became to others—and the more effective I became as a leader.

The Legacy I Want to Leave

If I walk away tomorrow, it won't be the reports or revenue spikes that define me.

It'll be the people.

The reps who went from surviving to thriving. The leaders who discovered they could build a career and a life. The managers who found their voice and learned how to help others find theirs.

The ripple effect.

If I can teach one person how to lead better, think smarter, and grow stronger—then they can teach two more. And those two become ten. And that's a legacy.

Not in metrics. But in momentum.

Harvard Business Review calls it "transformational leadership" —the kind that creates other leaders, not followers. The kind that multiplies. And I know that's what I've built. Because the people I've led are now leading others. Not in my shadow. But in their own light.

That's what matters. That's what lasts.

Because in the end, your legacy isn't who follows you—it's who no longer needs to.

They're not standing behind you in your shadow. They're leading beside someone else, in their own light. And that's leadership that echoes.

40

Purposeful

To really grieve… to walk with it, not just be crushed by it… you have to know who the hell you are.

And that right there? That was the hardest part for me.

Because for most of my life, I didn't know.

My identity was duct-taped to other people's expectations. Shaped by what they needed me to be. What I thought I had to be. There was maybe—maybe—a two-year window where who I was felt like mine. Unfiltered. Unshaped. Raw. And then? I shape-shifted my way through the rest.

When I was with Ashley, I molded myself to fit her family's blueprint. I trimmed off my rough edges to meet their conservative expectations. I adjusted what I said, what I wore, the music I liked, even what I ate. I said "yes" to things I wanted to scream "no" to. I became a product of survival—of blending in. Of contorting myself to stay needed.

I did it at work, too. Built myself in the image of what "successful leadership" looked like. Hit every metric, outperformed every goal, delivered every damn quarter, even when I was breaking inside.

But here's the thing no one tells you when you spend your life shapeshifting to survive that eventually, you lose track of your own reflection. You forget what your voice sounds like. You forget who you were before the molding started.

I think back to when I was a kid—before the masks—and I realize, I wasn't shy. I was just misunderstood. I was around adults most of the time, and I didn't know how to start conversations with other kids. So, they labeled me quiet. Timid. Antisocial. And I wore that label like it was truth. But the truth?

I just didn't know how to begin.

And even then, somewhere underneath all that, was a boy who was already storytelling. My great grandma used to call me "Preacher Boy." I'd spin these wild, imaginative tales—full plots, characters, conflict, climax, all of it—just off the top of my head. I'd perform for my family like I was on stage. No filter. No fear. Just raw imagination, poured into every room I walked into.

That version of me… that's the one I had to find again.

Because to grieve, to really navigate the tides of grief without letting it drown you—you have to know your own damn story. You have to know what you value. Because values become your compass when the storm rolls in. And grief? Grief is an ocean that doesn't ask for permission.

So, I built my compass. Slowly, meticulously, and reaching through the history of my life.

And these are my true norths:

1. Help Others.

I don't just like helping people—I need to. I run toward crisis. Toward fire. Toward chaos. People know that about me. They know I show up when shit hits the fan. They know I can be counted on. And I'm proud of that. It's not a savior complex. It's just… purpose.

2. Communication.

There's a phrase I used to teach my teams: Where are the blueberries?

Back in caveman days, when survival was the goal, if someone found food and didn't share that info? People died. Families starved. But if you communicated—if you said, "The blueberries are east, by the river"—your tribe lived. Communication is the reason humanity is still here.

And today, it's no different.

If you're hoarding information, you're letting people starve. If you're silent in your relationships, in your leadership, in your grief—you're letting your people starve.

I've seen what communication can do. It heals. It promotes. It elevates entire families. It builds leaders. And for me… it's personal. Because there are days when my daughter, who's almost school age now, still can't say much. But when she waves? When she blows a kiss? When she says "Dad"—even if it's once every few weeks—those moments matter more than anything else in the world.

3. Accountability.

Own your shit.

If you screw up—say it. If someone else is screwing up and you care about them—tell them. Don't sugarcoat. Don't coddle. Don't lie. Because the moment you start lying to yourself, you lose the map. And you can't survive grief without a damn map.

4. Loyalty.

Loyalty is the currency of connection.
Trust doesn't just happen. It's earned, tested, stretched, and earned again.

Whether it's marriage, friendship, parenting, or leading—when you give your word, you better mean it. I do.

Those values? They were forged in fire. I keep them in my heart to help me stay on course while navigating grief. They came from living. From loss. From everything I've crawled through.

So who am I?

I'm Dan. I'm a father to five kids on Earth—and two walk with me in my heart. I grew up broke. Knew how to stretch a dollar until it begged for mercy. I'm a veteran. A multi-unit leader. A husband. A friend. A son. I carry grief like a shadow—not to be rid of, but to walk with.

I've battled depression, betrayal, isolation, and rage. I've known the pain of divorce, of burying babies, of saying goodbye to the only person who ever truly understood me. But I've also known rebirth. Love. Connection. Redemption.

I'm a comic book nerd. I love physics, even if I don't understand all of it. I debate for fun. I coach for passion. I lead because I believe people deserve someone who gives a damn.

I'm not a Wall Street genius. I'm not some Ivy League scholar. But I am a man who knows how to lead hearts, not just teams. A man who loves Marvel™, laughs awkwardly, and still dreams like the kid who used to tell stories in his grandma's living room.

And why did I write this?

Because my brother, Travis, once told me, "There's no book for this kind of thing." My other brother, Bobby, told me, "Maybe you had to go through this… so the rest of us would know how to."

And that stuck.

I didn't write this to inspire. I didn't write it to sell. I wrote it because I had to. Because my story—raw, messy, uncut—was helping people. People kept calling. Kept reaching out. And I realized… this is what being purposeful feels like.

I don't believe everyone has a clear-cut purpose. But I believe in being purposeful.

And if sharing my story helps someone else crawl out of the dark— Helps a father hold on. Helps a leader lead through loss. If it helps someone stay alive one more day.

Then this was worth it.

Because if there's one thing, I know for sure is that …

Death fucking sucks.
But life?
Life is fucking beautiful.

www.ingramcontent.com/pod-product-compliance
Lightning Source LLC
Chambersburg PA
CBHW021707120626
46545CB00004B/1441